Understanding Your Business Clients

ABA FUNDAMENTALS

Understanding Your Business Clients

Bert Spector

AMERICAN BAR ASSOCIATION
Defending Liberty
Pursuing Justice

Cover design by Tamara Kowalski/ABA Publishing.

The materials contained herein represent the opinions of the authors and editors, and should not be construed to be the views or opinions of the law firms or companies with whom such persons are in partnership with, associated with, or employed by, nor of the American Bar Association unless adopted pursuant to the bylaws of the Association.

Nothing contained in this book is to be considered as the rendering of legal advice for specific cases, and readers are responsible for obtaining such advice from their own legal counsel. This book is intended for educational and informational purposes only.

Printed in the United States of America

17 16 15 14 13 5 4 3 2 1

Library of Congress Cataloging-in-Publication Data

Spector, Bert.
  ABA fundamentals : understanding your business clients / by Bert Spector.—
First Edition.
      pages cm
  Includes bibliographical references and index.
  ISBN 978-1-61438-830-2 (print)
  1. Corporation law—United States 2. Commercial law—United States. 3. Corporations—United States. I. Title.
  KF1414.85 .S+
  650.024'34—dc23

                                                    2012043779

Discounts are available for books ordered in bulk. Special consideration is given to state bars, CLE programs, and other bar-related organizations. Inquire at Book Publishing, ABA Publishing, American Bar Association, 321 North Clark Street, Chicago, Illinois 60654-7598.

www.ShopABA.org

TABLE OF CONTENTS

PREFACE

ABA Fundamentals: Understanding Your Business Clients is a book about business for lawyers; those who are currently working in-house and in various business-related practices, as well as those who are considering the practice of business law. It is not a text on business law. Those texts are plentiful and readily available. Instead, this is a guided tour through the world of your current or potential clients, and the narrative is offered from a business perspective rather than a legal one.

Let me explain what I mean. Business law texts are typically organized around legal concepts: contracts, torts, property law, and so forth. That makes perfect sense as a way to sort through the many legal issues faced by in-house and outside counsel. It is not, however, how corporate executives approach their own world. To help your interactions with those current and potential future clients, *Understanding Your Business Clients* is organized around concepts and issues that arise in the day-to-day activities of managers: finance, strategy, human resources, marketing, and so forth.

There are case examples presented in *Understanding Your Business Clients,* but not the kind typically offered in legal texts. Rather than court cases, I've offered illustrations from the world of business: quarterly financial reports from IBM, corporate structure at Disney, customer segmentation at Zara, hiring practices at Patagonia, to name just a few. These examples are offered to help illuminate and ground the many concepts offered in the text.

I've written the book based on the assumption that to represent a client most effectively, counsel needs to understand the underlying structure and function of the client's business. For in-house counsel, this understanding is critical in forging a partnership with the company's executives in order to best represent the interests of the corporation. For outside counsel, an appreciation of the context of business is critical in representing—and retaining—a firm's valuable corporate clients.

Understanding Your Business Clients is not meant to be a "mini" or "portable" MBA. Instead, based on my interaction with law firms— teaching business concepts to partners and associates and engaging in strategic consulting with large and boutique firms—I have selected topics where the services of counsel—both transaction and litigation services— are most likely to intersect with the activities of executives.

The book starts by covering key business functions, with separate chapters devoted to finances, business strategy, the corporation, human resource management, marketing, and corporate governance. Then, I delve into matters that generate a richness of legal transactions and, occasionally, litigation: risk management, compliance, intellectual property, mergers and acquisitions, and initial public offerings.

In truth, that distinction is somewhat artificial. Take marketing. This is a topic that is fundamental to any business as it attempts to create, serve, and retain customers. At the same time, marketing activities generate many legal issues that require counsel: anti-monopoly and anti-competitive practices, product liability, regulations on promotions, concerns about privacy, and so forth. Just like all the topics covered in *Understanding Your Business Clients*, marketing represents a conflux of business and legal activities.

To expedite the tour, I've built several features into the text:

- **Back of the Envelope Notes** present brief summaries of the key points.

- **Good to Know** offers a deeper dive into many of the issues raised in the chapter.

- **Point of Order** explores the particular legal implications of the topic under discussion.

The text concludes with a **Talking the Talk** appendix that provides a quick reference guide to the specialized vocabulary of business.

The goal of *Understanding Your Business Clients* is to make the world of your client accessible, understandable, and meaningful.

ACKNOWLEDGMENTS

A number of my colleagues at Northeastern University College of Business Administration provided important guidance and feedback to me as I wrote this book. Dennis Shaughnessy helped me to conceive and structure the text, and Don Margotta and Jeffery Born worked with me on the fine points of corporate finance and governance. Additionally, I would like to acknowledge and thank the following colleagues: Maureen Kelleher, Harry Lane, Wes Marple, Deigan Morris, José Santos, Frank Spital, and Emery Trahan. Outside of academics, I would like to acknowledge Justin Bagdady, Robert Calnan, Gisela Margotta, Kayte Spector-Bagdady, Seymour Spector, and Tess Spector.

My thanks to Erin Nevius and Sandra Johnson at ABA Publishing; Whitney Thompson, Annie Beck, Eric Zeiter, and Aaron Kantor at Lachina Publishing Services; and Katie Wilson at CheckPROZ, LLC.

CHAPTER **1**

CORPORATE FINANCE

Capital flows into and out of every corporation. Customers buy products and services, banks loan money, and investors purchase stocks and bonds. All that occurs while the corporation keeps its daily operations going and invests in future growth. Making decisions about how to raise that capital and then spend, record, and report all resulting financial transactions requires experts: financial managers and accountants.

At the same time, it is difficult to imagine any significant interaction between corporate executives and legal counsel that does not touch upon some equally significant financial transaction. In these transactions, it is vital that all sides have a clear understanding of one another. Just as attorneys have a specialized vocabulary, financial managers and accountants often seem to be speaking their own language. "Weighted average cost of capital," "net present value," "retained earnings," and "generally accepted accounting practices" are just some of the many terms you are likely to run across in your day-to-day dealings. This chapter provides an overview of the topic of corporate finance designed to ease transactions between financial experts and counsel.

Managing Finances

How to raise capital and then spend it: these are the two matters that most concern financial managers. Let's look at each one in turn.

Sources of Capital

When we think of where a corporation gets its money, we tend to focus first on sales revenues: the money the firm generates by selling the goods and services it produces. Indeed, most organizations look to sales as their primary source of day-to-day operating capital. But the money required to grow and expand, to acquire and globalize, often comes from other sources. In addition to sales revenues, corporations raise capital by investing, selling ownership shares (equity), and borrowing (bank loans and bonds).

Good to Know

Corporations can be investors themselves, using cash to buy stocks and bonds in other companies. They do this both to raise capital and to develop partnerships with these other companies.

Corporations raise capital by selling ownership in the form of stock. Investors buy stock in hopes that the value will rise. They also expect an annual dividend that the company may pay on each share from its net income. Corporations sell two kinds of stock: preferred and common. Preferred stock is, from the perspective of the buyer, a safer investment than common stock. The value of preferred stock remains steady and has a higher claim than common stock on any dividend that the company may pay. Also, preferred stock has a higher priority claim on liquidated assets should the firm declare bankruptcy. Perhaps the most important difference between preferred and common stock is that preferred stock confers no voting rights on the owner, while common stock does.

Good to Know

Dividends are declared at the discretion of the board of directors. Between 1995 and 2012, Apple's board declined to declare a dividend for shareholders. That span covered some difficult years for the corporation, but even as Apple recovered and then performed remarkably well, the board preferred to hold onto the cash in order to invest in projects and acquisitions. Given the growth in Apple's stock price, most investors were content. In March 2012, with over $100 billion in the company's cash stockpile, Apple's board broke the 17-year streak and declared a quarterly dividend.

Debt provides another source of capital through bank loans (referred to as notes) and the issuance of corporate bonds. Both notes and bonds require that the corporation pay interest in return for the use of capital. Because that interest—as well as the rate of repayment on the loans—is agreed to at the outset, debt is a highly predictable source of capital.

In addition to predictability, debt financing has other important advantages over selling stock for a corporation. A shareholder is an owner of the corporation, while a bond holder is a creditor. Debt does not provide the lender any direct voice in the operation of the corporation: banks and bond owners do not get a vote in corporate affairs.[1] In addition, the government subsidizes debt financing by allowing corporations to deduct interest on their tax returns.

The major disadvantage of debt financing compared to equity sales is that loans and bonds require the corporation to pay back in the predetermined manner. Shareholders expect annual payouts in the form of dividends, of course, but there is no legal requirement that the corporation declare a dividend. In difficult times, the dividend can simply be scrubbed. Shareholders may be upset with that decision, but the firm itself will not be in immediate danger of defaulting on loans.

Point of Order

Virtually anyone can become a shareholder. However, because stock ownership is a contract between the holder and the issuer, it must be entered into knowingly and voluntarily.

Point of Order

The sale of securities—stocks, bonds, and other financial instruments—by corporations is regulated by both federal and state laws. Applicable state statutes are referred to as *blue-sky laws*.

Point of Order

Prohibitions against "insider trading" of securities cover situations in which the trader is in possession of material, nonpublic information. Although typically applied to board members and company executives, "insiders" might also include outside counsel, financial journalists, financial printers, or—in one instance—a psychiatrist who gained access to inside information from a patient. Insiders are allowed to sell their company stock. Corporate officers, however, must disclose such sales to the U.S. Securities and Exchange Commission (SEC).

---

1.   There is no denying that holders of significant debt can exert influence even without a direct vote. That influence expands if the corporation declares bankruptcy.

Point of Order

Federal law does not explicitly define a security; rather, it offers examples, some specific (stocks, bonds, notes), others more general ("investment contract," which includes—as defined by subsequent case law—futures, certificates, swaps, and debentures).

But what happens when a firm cannot pay back the debt it has accumulated through bank loans and bond sales? The firm faces a number of difficult choices. Executives will try to restructure the debt by negotiating with holders of debt. In extreme circumstances, firms will need to declare bankruptcy. Given that there are advantages and disadvantages to all types of financing, well-managed firms use a mix of stocks, bonds, and loans.

Good to Know

To guide potential corporate bond purchasers, rating agencies such as Moody's and Standard and Poor's, which are registered with and recognized by the SEC, rate bonds issued from various corporations according to the risk that the purchaser faces. The greater the risk caused by uncertainty both within the company and in the company's competitive environment, the higher the interest rate purchasers will expect and, as a result, the more expensive it will be for the company to raise capital. When the rating falls to the lowest levels, corporate bonds are referred to as "high-yield bonds" (or "junk bonds"), which promise high interest for high risk. Banks, too, rely on these rating agencies to determine how much interest to charge for loans.

Good to Know

Although individuals are allowed to purchase corporate bonds, it is almost entirely an activity dominated by large financial institutions. Individuals are more likely to participate in the secondary market, buying from institutions that purchased at the time the bond was issued. Given the risks involved in the secondary bond market, however, as well as the complexity of calculations, third parties are typically used to broker such sales.

How to Spend Capital

When it comes to making decisions concerning what to do with capital, no requirement is more fundamental to a financial manager—the chief financial officer (CFO) of an organization and his/her expert staff—than to think like an investor. Firms count on capital markets—banks and stock and bond purchasers—to provide money through loans and purchases of ownership. The capital markets determine how to allocate resources based on expected return and reliability/safety of the investment.

Every financial decision made by a corporation will be scrutinized by investors and analysts. How effective is the company at investing *my* money? If investors come to believe that they would be better off placing their money elsewhere, then a valuable source of capital will dry up. Either that or the cost of capital—how much return the company will have to offer to raise money—will rise. Or both.

The requirement to think and act as an investor leads to three underlying principles that help guide decision-making: never forget about opportunity costs, pay attention to the cost of capital, and look forward and account for the time value of money.

Pay Attention to Opportunity Cost. Part of the equation that figures into any investor's decision-making is: How much more would I be making if I invested my capital differently? In order to think like an investor, financial managers also look at opportunity cost. Every decision made involves possibilities rejected and opportunities foregone. There are always alternative decisions an investor can make. Investors will test any course of action against the next best alternative—the opportunity cost—and so should executives.

Here's a quick example. Keeping cash on hand is important to a corporation because cash is a liquid asset that can be used in an emergency to make short-term payments. That's valuable. But for every dollar kept as cash, there is an opportunity missed to invest that dollar and receive a return on that investment. Cash can also be distributed to shareholders in the form of dividends, thus providing shareholders with the opportunity to invest that money on their own. Opportunity cost looks at the next best alternative use of capital: the decision *not* taken.

Good to Know

My colleague Professor Diegan Morris uses this example to explain opportunity cost to students: assume that an aunt has died and left you with an original Picasso. How much, he asks, would it cost you to hang the artwork? Students are not expected to give amounts, just the categories that would make up the cost. After listing categories ranging from a picture hook to lighting, security, and insurance, the professor notes they are missing the most significant category. "You could *sell* the bloody painting for $20 million! That $20 million is the opportunity cost of hanging it." That's a vital lesson for all to follow.

Weigh the Cost of Capital. Corporations, as we have seen, raise capital from a number of sources: customers, to be sure, but also investors and lenders. And it always costs money to raise money. Different sources of capital—bank loans, bonds, equity, and so forth—have different costs; that is, different interest rates associated with them.

Every company needs to understand its cost of capital: How much does it have to spend in order to receive capital? The most important calculation is weighted average cost of capital, which looks at the cost of each source of money and the proportion of the firm's total capital coming from those sources.

Look Forward and Account for the Time Value of Money. Looking forward requires that only the future implications of a decision be considered. Sunk costs are not folded into financial decision-making. What the company has already spent—its sunk costs—is past and cannot be undone. As I will discuss later in this chapter, accountants need to look backward in order to report to investors and regulators on what has occurred in the last reporting period. But a different set of rules applies to financial managers. What is important to financial managers is only what happens in the future as a result of today's decision: future cash flow.

But how much is future cash flow worth? The only way to answer that question is to take into account the passage of time and determine the net present value of money.

Let's say an executive faces a decision on whether to spend $1 million on a project. The expected cash flow from that project is $4 million to be received over a 5-year period. Sounds like an excellent return. However, the time value of money tells us that the $4 million payment spread out over 5 years will be worth less than $4 million in today's dollars. So what is the net present value (NPV) of the $4 million received over 5 years; that is, the value of that $4 million in current dollars? To derive that figure, experts use complex formulas to discount future cash flows based on time periods and other considerations. The NPV of this investment can then be compared to the NPV that will be derived from other projects that are competing for the same $1 million up-front investment.

These principles—opportunity costs, weighted cost of capital, and the time value of money—are used to guide financial decision-making in organizations. Once decisions are made and financial transactions occur, they must be accounted for and reported. How, exactly, did those transactions impact on the bottom line of the corporation and the returns that shareholders expect on their investment? To answer these questions, corporations turn to the practice of accounting.

Accounting for Performance

A July 2012 headline in the *New York Times* read: "IBM Posts Strong Quarter Despite Softness in Revenue." CEO Virginia Rometty announced that revenues had dropped 3 percent from the previous year. So with sales down, what exactly made this a "strong" performance? Well, Rometty noted, earnings were up. And that was considered to be good news coming from one of the United States' largest multinational corporations.

How do we account for this apparent anomaly, revenues are down while earnings are up? "Account for" is exactly the right term, because accounting is the method by which a corporation—and investors—measures its performance. Accountants quantify every aspect of a corporation's financial performance. That accounting, in turn, allows analysts to work those numbers through various formulae and ratios to offer guidance to both managers intent on improving performance and investors intent on making wise decisions. Accountants also supply the data that becomes part of the various reports required by the SEC for public companies. We will look in greater detail at those compliance requirements in Chapter 7. For now, we should understand just how accounting records, analyzes, and reports a company's financial transactions.

General Accounting Principles

Accounting looks not just at the performance of a corporation, but at all the available financial activities and resources. How able is a company to pay its bills, keep its operations going, and invest in the future? In the case of IBM, what portion of each dollar of revenue actually made it to the bottom line? Every significant question in a company relating to how money is spent will be recorded, reported, and analyzed through the accounting process. It is no surprise, then, that accounting is often said to be the "language of business."

The question of how to record and report financial dealings is complex, often involving judgment about how, where, and when to enter a transaction. Poor judgment can undermine a corporation's financial integrity, dilute investor and creditor confidence, and—at the extreme—place a firm in legal jeopardy. To help ensure that these judgments align with the expectations of investors and regulators, accountants in the United States follow a common set of principles, the generally accepted accounting principles (GAAP), created by the Financial Accounting Standards Board (FASB) with input from the American Institute of Certified Public Accountants (AICPA).

Good to Know

For most government entities—state, county, and local governmental units, but *not* the federal government—accounting standards are set by the Governmental Accounting Standards Board (GASB). The federal government follows the Federal Accounting Standards Advisory Board (FASAB) principles.

Good to Know

There is a good deal of pressure on the SEC to move away from GAAP and adopt the International Financial Reporting Standards (IFRS), a global accounting standard. Many large U.S.-based corporations already use IFRS for their international operations and subsidiaries.

Following these principles, a corporation will produce a number of financial statements. For multi-business corporations, the reports represent a consolidation of the appropriate transactions and activities within the various units. For our purposes here, let's look at three significant ones: the balance sheet, the income statement, and the statement of cash flows.

Income Statement. If you are looking for the "bottom line" of a business's performance, the income statement is the place to go. It surprises people to learn, however, that the bottom line is referred to not as "profit" but as "net income." That term, net income, refers to a company's revenues adjusted for the cost of doing business and other expenses. In the IBM example, revenue was down. But because expenses were lowered during the quarter at an even greater rate than the revenue fell, net income increased.

Good to Know

Like virtually all accounting figures, net income calculates performance during a specified time period: a quarter or a year. An exception is retained earnings, which is a measure of all the firm's earnings since its inception.

Revenue refers to payments received or expected in exchange for goods and services delivered. Revenue is *not* the same as cash. Two accounting rules explain the revenue/cash distinction. The first is the rule of accrual accounting, which says that the economic impact of a transaction is recorded when the transactional contract is agreed to rather than when the cash is received. Added to that are rules concerning revenue recognition; that is, when sales are recorded for accounting purposes.

Revenue is "recognized" when the company performs its side of the exchange—goods delivered, services rendered—and the customer agrees to make payment. Revenue recognition does not imply that the corporation has received full payment from the customer. Goods or services may be delivered in Quarter 1, and the company and its customer may agree to payment in Quarter 2. Under the rules of accounting, the revenue would be recognized in Quarter 1 because there is a reasonable expectation that payment will be received and a clear, agreed-upon schedule for when it will be received.

Point of Order

In legal terms, revenue recognition occurs when a contract that contains both present undertakings and a commitment to future conduct of the parties has been agreed to.

Point of Order

Corporations often prepare *pro forma* statements to demonstrate the expected return on investment (ROI) from significant projects, including new equipment, new property, and acquisitions. A *pro forma* does not need to follow GAAP. It is intended to give a truer picture of projected earnings than a typical accounting calculation. But beware: The SEC says that using *pro forma* to obscure GAAP results constitutes fraud.

Good to Know

Revenue recognition can be a tricky business and, in the wrong hands, open to fraud. In what many still consider to be the largest accounting fraud case in U.S. history, the now-defunct energy supplier Enron adopted revenue recognition practices that greatly and fraudulently inflated its income. The total value of uncertain and ambiguous deals—often stretching over 30 years—was booked at the time of the contract. Enron's tactics stretched the limits of "reasonable expectation" to the point of being fanciful. The fact that Enron's many questionable accounting practices were approved by its accounting firm, Arthur Andersen, led directly to the demise of both Enron and Arthur Andersen, jail sentences for a number of Enron executives, passage of the Sarbanes-Oxley Act (SOX), and a tightening of rules by the SEC.

For this reason, the question of how much cash a corporation has available at any given moment cannot be answered by looking at revenue. Cash is important in determining such questions as liquidity and solvency. Analysts interested in gaining insight into a corporation's cash position will need to look at the statement of cash flow, which will be covered below. But first let's look at the balance sheet.

Balance Sheet. The balance sheet—a snapshot of the corporation's financial position in any given period of time—shows what a company has, what it owes, and what it is worth. The balance sheet is based on what is known as "the accounting equation":

$$\text{Assets} = \text{liabilities} + \text{shareholders' equity}$$

Assets refer to the value of a firm's holdings—both tangible, such as equipment, property, and inventory, and intangible, such as intellectual property—that can reasonably be expected to be either converted into cash or used productively by the corporation. Liabilities refer to obligations the corporation has to make payments. Shareholders' equity is the difference between assets and liabilities; that is, shareholders' remaining interest in the corporation once all debts are paid off.

Good to Know

In August 2012, in an effort to "clean up" its books, Hewlett-Packard announced an $8 billion write-down on one of its assets. Firms write down assets that have diminished in market value over time. A write-down is a "paper" loss that reduces net income and, as a result, lowers the corporation's tax burden for that period. In the Hewlett-Packard case, the company had purchased an asset—Electronic Data Systems (EDS)—for $13.9 billion in 2008. Four years later, accountants valued that asset at less than $6 billion based on the disappointing revenues it had generated. Hence, the write-down.

The fundamental principle of the accounting equation is that, at the conclusion of the recording of every transaction, the equation will remain in balance. Therefore, every transaction affects at least two elements of the equation—hence the term "double-entry bookkeeping." When a company borrows money from a bank, for instance, both assets and liabilities will increase. If the liability increases by a greater amount than the asset, then the shareholders' equity must decrease accordingly. The main point of the accounting equation is that it must *always* be in balance.

Statement of Cash Flows. As mentioned earlier, revenue and cash are not the same. Revenue is booked when a sale is made and payment is agreed to, not when cash flows into the corporation. It is the statement of cash flows that shows the amount of cash collected and paid out, and accounts for how a company actually used its cash. The statement of cash flows helps answer questions such as from where the corporation generated cash (remember from earlier in this chapter, there are multiple sources), how it used cash, and how the cash balance changed. The statement can also be used to assess the liquidity position of the corporation to determine if it can generate the cash required to meet its current liabilities.

The major advantage of cash, of course, is liquidity. The ability to turn an asset into cash quickly and with low transaction costs defines how liquid an asset is. A large real estate holding may be quite valuable but is not terribly liquid; it can take months to sell, and there will be high transaction costs in making that sale. Cash is a completely liquid asset.

But how much cash should a corporation have? At a minimum, enough to meet day-to-day needs. Silicon Valley companies tend to keep more cash on hand than other companies, perhaps as a hedge against the volatility of the industry. Also, corporations can use cash to make strategic acquisitions.[2]

Corporations may also use cash to buy back their own stock from current shareholders (referred to as a stock repurchase or a share buyback). They do so for one or more of the following reasons:

- It is a way of returning excess cash to shareholders. The same cash could be used to pay dividends, of course. However, for the shareholder, the money gained by selling stock back to the issuing corporation (a capital gain) is taxed at a lower rate than income received in the form of a dividend.

- Reducing the number of available shares on the open market should raise the value of each remaining share.

- The corporation may believe that its stock is currently undervalued by the market. The buyback should drive the value up to the point where the corporation can resell the stock.

The stock may either be cancelled or held for future resale as treasury stock. Because a corporation cannot own itself, treasury stock does not confer the right to vote or receive a dividend. A buyback must be reported in the Statement of Shareholders' Equity as part of the corporation's 10K filing with the SEC.

Too much cash can be a problem as well. Remember the concept of opportunity costs? If the firm holds too much cash, it is giving up the opportunity to invest that cash in new ventures or to distribute the cash to stockholders in the form of dividends. The question of how much cash to have is a judgment call that can generate some differences between managers on one hand and shareholders on the other.

Ratio Analysis

Investors gain insight into a corporation's operations by using the data provided by the various financial statements to calculate ratios concerning profitability, utilization of assets, liquidity, and debt burden. Earnings per share (EPS), which corporations are required to report, divides the

---

2. Acquisitions can be done with cash, stock, or some combination of the two. For a further discussion, see Chapter 9.

company's net income by the number of common shares it has sold. That metric indicates the profit behind each share of common stock. Investors will typically calculate earnings before interest, taxes, depreciation, and amortization (EBITDA), which is helpful in comparing one corporation's financial performance to another's. The ratio EBITDA as a percent of sales can compare corporations even across industries (the higher the better). Investors will also look at profit margins (net income divided by net sales), return on assets (net income divided by total assets), and return on equity as additional indicators of financial performance. These and other ratios used in financial analysis are described in Exhibit 1-1.

Exhibit 1-1: Key Analytic Ratios

Ratio:	Calculated by:	Meaning:
Earnings per share (EPS)	Net income ÷ number of shares	Understand profit behind each share
Profit margin	Net income ÷ revenue	Compare how much profit is generated by selling different goods/ services
Return on assets (ROA)	Net income ÷ total assets	Analyze how well a company converts investments into profits
Return on equity (ROE)	Net income ÷ equity	Analyze how effectively a company is producing shareholder wealth
Liquidity ratio	Current assets ÷ current liabilities	Analyze ability of firm to pay short-term obligations
Debt-to-total assets (expressed as a %)	Total debts ÷ total assets	Assess how much debt the company is using to finance growth

Taken together, these financial statements constitute a significant portion of the filings required of public companies by the SEC. I will analyze the reporting and compliance requirements in Chapter 7. All financial statements are intended to provide investors—both current and potential—as well as regulators and managers with a clear and thorough accounting of the performance of the company, its use of assets to generate returns, and its financial health.

Finally—Why Corporate Finance Matters

Financial transactions reside at the core of any corporation. Therefore, questions regarding how to raise capital, spend money, and record transactions will be raised in virtually every significant activity that occurs. The legal regulatory environment in which these activities occur will be covered in Chapter 7. The point of this chapter is to introduce the frameworks and vocabulary used by executives to understand their own business and to explain that business to investors and other business partners, including in-house and outside counsel.

Back of the Envelope Notes

Key sources of capital:
- Sales revenues
- Sale of equity (stocks)
- Borrowing (loans, bonds)
- Return on investments

....

Dividends—which represent a current return on a shareholder's investment—are paid at the discretion of the board; there is no legal obligation to declare a dividend.

....

In order to think like an investor, financial managers need to:
1. Pay attention to opportunity costs.
2. Weigh the cost of capital.
3. Look forward and account for the time value of money.

....

The time value of money suggests that money is worth more today than the same amount of money will be in the future. Executives need to assure themselves that giving up money today for money in the future will pay off.

....

To analyze the future cash flows that will be generated by any decision, managers need to discount that cash flow by how much time it will take to reap the expected benefits and factors—including inflation—that will reduce the value of cash flow. That calculation—discounted cash flow—allows executives to understand future benefits in terms of today's dollars: the net present value of that cash flow.

....

Generally accepted accounting principles are established by the Financial Accounting Standards Board with input from the American Institute of Certified Public Accountants.

....

Revenue and cash are not the same. For accounting purposes, revenue is booked at the time the transaction is agreed upon by the parties, the products and/or services are delivered, and the terms of payment are specified. But revenue does not become cash until the payment is actually received. Therefore, corporations can have healthy revenues but still have a cash flow problem while they await payment.

....

Every entry into the balance sheet must impact at least two of the elements of the accounting equation—assets, liabilities, and/or shareholder equity—in order to maintain balance.

....

Corporations need to keep enough cash on hand to be able to pay bills and maintain day-to-day operations. They may also accumulate cash as a hedge against market volatility and to increase their ability to make acquisitions. However, cash is a non-earning asset. Corporations that keep too much cash on hand may be passing up too many opportunities to invest that money and generate a return.

CHAPTER **2**

BUSINESS STRATEGY

"Strategy" is a term you will hear regularly in your interaction with business clients. By itself, strategy is not a legal concept. Rather, it is the big-picture story of how a business will compete, grow, and make a profit. It refers to the long-term position of the business. All transactions you may undertake with a business client, from setting employment contracts to negotiating mergers and acquisitions, will occur within the context of that business's strategy. Understanding what that strategy is and how it works to enhance the performance of the company can be helpful.

The Basics of Business Strategy

At a basic level, all businesses must answer three questions about themselves: *who, what,* and *how.* The choices a business makes in each of these questions make up the building blocks of its business strategy.[1] The *who* question identifies the business's target market, the *what* explains the product/service offer the business is making to the marketplace, and the *how* identifies the firm's business model, which is the way it delivers its *what* to its *who* in an efficient, effective, and—ultimately—profitable way.

---

1. I am separating *business* strategy from *corporate* strategy. The role and strategic goals of the corporation will be discussed in Chapter 3.

Who/What/How

Let's start our consideration of business strategy with what it is that the company sells: the strategic *what* of a company. This may seem like a relatively straightforward matter: we sell computers, we offer legal services, we sell clothing. However, understanding a business's strategic *what* can be, and often is, more complicated.

Take McDonald's. What is it selling? A simple answer would be: burgers, fries, Coke, and milk shakes. Although that answer is correct, it is far from complete. McDonald's also sells convenience, speed, consistency, and reliability. When you stop at a McDonald's, you know exactly what to expect. You know the Big Mac you get at a McDonald's in Dayton, Ohio will be exactly the same as the Big Mac at the Arlington, Virginia McDonald's. And you know that you'll be served quickly. All of these elements—the tangible burger as well as intangible elements such as speed and consistency—are part of the McDonald's *what.*

Good to Know

In discussing the McDonald's *what,* I used Coke purposefully. Like many restaurant chains, McDonald's signs "exclusivity" contracts with suppliers; in this case, Coca-Cola. Exclusivity gives McDonald's better financial terms with its supplier, although it also limits the scope of what it can offer customers. No Pepsi with your fries at McDonald's. Negotiating the optimal contract with suppliers is part of the *how* of business strategy.

Point of Order

Products often come with an express warranty, which is a statement of fact and/or promise that the seller makes about the product. Products also come with an implied warranty, which is an implicit promise by a merchant that the goods are reasonably fit for the purpose for which they are being sold.

Selecting a target market for those products and services adds a second key dimension to a business's strategy: its *who.* Why do businesses need to define their target market? Won't they sell to any customer willing to buy? Of course. But a good strategy typically targets a particular set of customers to understand their needs and find products and services for which they will be willing to pay.[2] A business may define its *who* broadly or narrowly, but if the definition of *who* is too broad—that is, the business tries to attract *every*body—it may end up pleasing *no*body.

---

2. I will discuss approaches to segmenting the market in Chapter 5.

Businesses that define their customer base too broadly may find themselves unable to appeal to any particular market. Focused businesses—that is, focused on a specific *who*—can develop a sharper understanding of customers and their tastes. In the fashion industry, we can see this with, say, Abercrombie & Fitch. Those of us who are not young teenagers may walk into any Abercrombie store and make a purchase, but we know we are not the target market. Everything from its product design and mix to store design and types of employees is meant to attract a particular type of customer.

The need to define a target market segment may be especially obvious in the retailing business, but it is applied in other industries as well. Is this company selling to individuals (business-to-consumer, or "B2C") or to businesses? If it is selling to businesses (known as "B2B," or business-to-business), then which businesses? Corporations may, of course, have multiple answers to these questions. We want to sell to *both* individuals *and* businesses. We want to sell *both* to large corporations *and* to governments. In these cases, corporations will often create separate divisions, each pursuing its own target market.

Point of Order

Statutes covering contracts for selling products and services to customers vary widely from state to state. To bring some uniformity to those statutes, the National Conference of Commissioners on Uniform State Laws and the American Law Institute created the Uniform Commercial Code. The Commission and the Law Institute will, from time to time, lobby to bring state laws into greater uniformity.

It's easy for companies to become focused on, and excited about, their *what* and *who*—their product and market. In the last decade, a great deal of attention has been paid to the company's *how*—its business model. Think about a business as a bundle of activities: purchasing raw materials, designing products, making those products, selling and delivering them to customers, providing after-sales service, and so forth. These activities and the linkages among them make up a firm's business model.

One of the key business model design decisions involves determining who will perform each of the activities. Not all business model activities, after all, will be performed by the company itself. Some are likely to be outsourced; that is, performed by a completely separate company under a contractual arrangement. Everything from managing information systems and providing legal counsel to running the employees' cafeteria and managing the parking garage can be outsourced.

Deciding where business model activities will be performed—specifically, in what country—is another important strategic choice. In the case of offshoring, the company takes an activity that had previously been performed in its home country and moves it to another country. That choice is typically made to lower labor costs. Although it happens less frequently, a company may choose to onshore an activity: that is, take an activity that had been performed outside of the company's home country and move it back to that country.

Strategic Innovation

Strategy is not meant to change daily, monthly, or even annually. At the same time, strategy is not meant to be forever. Businesses change their strategies over time, often in response to changes in the competitive environment but also as a result of new technologies (think about how the Internet triggered sweeping alterations in the strategy of many businesses), new customer awareness (for example, customers wanting to "go green"), or even new leadership (a new CEO wanting to make his/her mark by moving the company in a different direction). A business that changes its strategy frequently is probably in trouble; a business that holds onto its old strategy too long is also likely to create problems for itself.

The term strategic innovation refers to significant alterations in a business's *who/what/how* choices. Admittedly, the term "significant" is not terribly specific. Still, there is a distinction to be drawn between significant change—strategic innovation—and incremental change.

Good businesses will make incremental improvements constantly. However, there will be times when incremental change is insufficient, even harmful, to the competitive position of a business. Businesses wedded to a particular technology, product, and/or market often find it difficult to respond to disruptions in the world around them. Borders, a bookseller that stuck with physical stores and printed books while Amazon and Barnes & Noble invested in e-readers, declared bankruptcy in 2011.

Good to Know

To appreciate how incremental change can actually undo an entire industry faced with new technology, James Utterback tells the story about the 19th century ice barons of New England.[3] These were folks like Frederick Tudor, the "Ice King," who built fortunes by harvesting "natural" ice from frozen New England ponds and shipping it around the world. Through regular research and development (R&D) investment, Tudor and his contemporaries made incremental improvements in the processes—the *how* of their strategy—for storing and shipping ice.

Skip ahead to the 1870s when experimentation with machine-made ice began to show promising results. Electric refrigerators were another 50 years in the future, but the direction of the ice business seemed clear. Natural ice would soon be replaced by "machine-made" ice. Ice barons would need to engage in strategic innovation in order to survive: switch R&D investment away from finding more efficient ways of packing and shipping naturally harvested ice and invest instead in the up-and-coming ice-making technology. Obvious, right? Well, apparently not. The New England ice barons reacted to these innovations by redoubling their investments in incremental improvements in the harvesting, storing, insulating, and shipping of natural ice. In that case, incremental improvements led them into extinction.

Strategic innovation starts with a thorough understanding of the dynamics of the competitive environment; that is, the world outside of the company itself. So, let's turn next to that concept.

---

3.   This example comes from James M. Utterback, *Mastering the Dynamics of Innovation: How Companies Can Seize Opportunities in the Face of Technological Change* (Boston: Harvard Business School Press, 1994).

Analyzing the Competitive Environment

No business operates in a vacuum. Forces outside the business will inevitably impact success and profitability, and any business that ignores those forces is destined to fail. When managers seek to assess the external environment, they typically call upon some framework to guide their diagnosis. Strategic diagnosis of the business's external environment often starts with a SWOT Analysis—Strengths, Weaknesses, Opportunities, and Threats.

Strengths and weaknesses look at the internal capabilities one business has compared to its competitors. Customer service, logistics, adaptability, marketing process—these are all attributes that companies can evaluate. What competencies do we possess that are better than our competitors'? These would be strengths. What are we not as good at as our competitors? That would be a weakness. Now, the company can build on its strengths and improve its weaknesses. Opportunities and threats look to the external environment to determine what favorable or unfavorable circumstances may exist. There may be opportunities to expand overseas, but there may also be a threat of significant foreign competitors entering a business's marketplace. Remember, these are not either/or choices. A thorough analysis should reveal weaknesses as well as strengths, threats as well as opportunities.

SWOT analysis is a technique for providing a quick overview of a business's strategic situation, and it has become quite popular. What it gains in simplicity, however, it lacks in analytic power. What is the relationship between strengths and opportunities, weaknesses and threats? And what does this analysis tell managers about the relative attractiveness of the industry in which they currently compete or that they may choose to enter? To provide a more rigorous analytic framework through which to view the competitive environment, most managers turn to Michael Porter's Five Forces framework.

Good to Know

In his research, Michael Porter noticed that some industries were more profitable over time than others. Between 1992 and 2006, for example, security brokers, soft drink makers, and advertising agencies returned the greatest profitability, while hotels, mail order businesses, and airlines were at the bottom of the list. He suggested that industry differences could be explained by the external factors that shaped each industry, and he developed his Five Forces model to understand those elements and interactions.

Exhibit 2-1: Porter's Five Forces

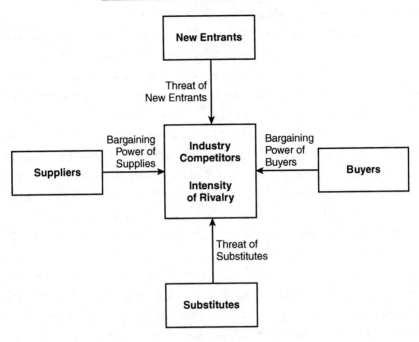

Porter also noticed that most managers focused almost exclusively on the state of competition within their industry. That is, they limited the scope of their analysis to direct competitors. However, four additional forces helped determine just how profitable an industry is (see Exhibit 2-1). Businesses need to appreciate the relative power of their suppliers as well as the buyers (customers) of their products. There are "threats" as well: new companies that can enter the industry and substitute products that might be offered by companies from other industries.

Suppliers have high bargaining power, for example, when there are only a few on which the entire industry must rely. Customers also can have high bargaining power if, for example, a single customer accounts for a large percentage of a business's sales. Walmart, as you can imagine, has a great deal of power as a buyer of consumer products—say, Gillette razor blades and Mars candies—from the manufacturers. The point is, the higher the power in any one of these five forces—greater supplier or customer bargaining power, intensity of rivalry or threats from new competitors and substitutes—the lower the overall profitability of the businesses in that industry. That analysis helps explain why airlines are so low on the profitability list, while the suppliers of the planes and parts—Boeing and GE Aviation, for example—enjoy more robust profits.

Porter also offered a more disciplined way of looking at threats to an industry. The two types of threats the framework highlights are the threats of new entrants to an industry and the threat of product substitution from outside the industry. How easy or difficult is it for competitors to enter and compete effectively in a particular industry? The capital requirements to start up may be prohibitive, making for a low threat. It would be difficult to raise the capital necessary to start a new automobile company, for instance. The capital requirements may be low, however. If one company started up a web page design company on a shoestring, why couldn't another one—or one hundred—do the same? In that case, the threat of new entrants would be quite high.

The threat of substitutions is typically more difficult to assess. It refers to a new industry with an offer that customers may prefer to the offers of a business's industry. When oleomargarine was first introduced, for example, it was more than a competitor for butter. It was a non-dairy product that challenged the market supremacy of a dairy-based product. Today, watch makers find themselves facing an unexpected product substitute as young consumers forgo watch purchases, relying instead on their cell phones for the same functionality.

Finally, the model looks at the state of rivalry within any given industry. Managers can start simply by taking a count of competitors, but there is much more to the analysis of rivalry. How big and dominant is the main player? How attached are customers to particular brands? How difficult is it for customers to switch from one competitor to another? The framework suggests that customers with lots of choices will shop for price bargains, placing greater pressure on incumbents to keep their costs low.

Five Forces is a framework for analyzing an industry, not a single business. In any given industry, even the most profitable ones, there will be winners and losers; some will do well and others will go out of business. Some businesses will develop an edge over others. To understand the sources of that edge, we need to turn to the concept of competitive advantage.

Competitive Advantage

The *who/what/how* framework is helpful in describing a business's strategy. Five Forces allows for an analysis of the relative attractiveness of an industry. But there is another key element that needs to be addressed. Competitive advantage is the notion of identifying what it is that separates one business from its competitors. What is it that makes our business attractive to customers? What is it that we have that our competitors do not?

Porter kicks off this discussion as well. Once businesses are clear about which industry they are in, they can then choose between what Porter labels generic strategies. Most particularly, he suggests, businesses can choose between a low-cost and a differentiated position. Selecting a low-cost position within an industry is exactly what it sounds like. Everything the company does—from the relationships it creates with suppliers to the internal logistics of the operation—is designed to a single end: keep costs down.

Businesses selling commodities—undifferentiated products ranging from corn to gas—are the most common examples of companies that place their emphasis on keeping costs as low as possible. In retailing, Walmart is the most obvious—and among the most successful—in claiming and maintaining a low-cost position. Through a relentless focus on keeping costs low, Walmart is able to set lower prices than competitors while maintaining a profitable bottom line.

Good to Know

A low-cost strategy is *not* the same as a low-price strategy. Any company can lower its prices, a least temporarily. That's just what Kmart did when it matched Walmart's prices in order to compete. However, without matching Walmart's ability to keep costs low, Kmart went bankrupt.

Businesses may instead decide to follow a differentiation position, one that emphasizes standing out from competitors more than low costs. For these companies, the primary attention will not be on low costs but rather on finding ways to make the business's products and services distinct. There are any number of strategic differentiators available: BMW has elegant engineering, Zara has speed to market, Amazon has customer service, Interface Global has environmental responsibility, and In-N-Out Burger has customization of fast food.

Note that I said differentiators do not place their *primary* strategic emphasis on low costs. No company can ignore cost pressures, of course.

Carlos Ghosn, CEO of Nissan and Renault, once said, "I don't see how one can manage a business without keeping one eye glued to expenses. It's a fantasy to think otherwise." The distinction between low cost and differentiation strategies is one of emphasis.

Finally—Why Business Strategy Matters

Through our discussions of the intricacies of strategy, we should not lose sight of its main purpose. Strategy tells a story, sets direction, and guides decision-making. As such, strategy is valuable to folks who work for the business. For people on the inside, strategy helps determine what opportunities to take advantage of and what opportunities may be beyond the scope of the business. Where will investments be made, opportunities exploited, and initiatives taken? To both in-house and outside counsel, strategy defines the basic context in which transactions occur.

Back of the Envelope Notes

The three building blocks of business strategy:
- *Who* is our customer (market)?
- *What* is the product or service we are selling (offer)?
- *How* do we deliver our product/service to our customer (business model)?

. . . .

A firm's business model is made up of activities such as purchasing, designing, making, delivering, and servicing that allow the firm to deliver its products to its customers.

. . . .

Outsourcing and offshoring are different:
- Outsourcing involves turning over some activities of a firm's business model to another company.
- Offshoring involves transferring some activities of a firm's business model to a subsidiary in another country.

The two are often combined when a company outsources an activity to a separate company in a foreign country.

. . . .

No strategy is permanent. Changing too frequently will confuse customers and employees. When a company sticks with a strategy for too long, it risks falling behind more innovative competitors.

• •

Businesses wedded to a particular technology, product, and/or market often find it difficult to respond to disruptions in the world around them.

• •

Companies need to regularly assess their own strengths and weaknesses as well as the opportunities and threats posed by a constantly shifting external environment.

• •

To understand the competitive dynamics in their industry, executives need to consider not just customers and competitors but also suppliers, as well as the threat of new industries luring away their current customers.

• •

Porter identified a number of generic competitive strategies, including:
- Low cost
- Differentiation

Businesses will attempt to do some of each but will tend to emphasize one over the other.

CHAPTER **3**

THE CORPORATION

Chapter 2 explored business strategy and competitive advantage. Let's now turn to the corporation: the legal entity responsible for the oversight of the business and the care of investors' money. It is the corporate level that attracts the direct involvement of both the in-house and outside counsel. The goal of this chapter is to provide an understanding of the complex structure and strategies of a corporation.

The Structure of the Corporation

The distinction between a business—which is a configuration of product/service (*what*), target market (*who*), and business model (*how*)—and a corporation may seem like one of semantics, especially when the corporation consists of a single business. Wawa, a convenience store chain in the Northeast, and In-N-Out Burger, a hamburger chain in the West, are examples of corporations that run a single business. In cases like these, the same executives will be performing both the corporate role and the business role.

But those examples are rare, and becoming more so. Today, most businesses exist in what we call a multi-business corporation. Exhibit 3-1 provides examples of multi-business corporations and the businesses they operate. In the multi-business corporation, a corporate center governs the corporation's divisions. The corporate center issues securities, allocates capital to the divisions, reports to federal and state agencies as well as to shareholders, makes merger and acquisition decisions, manages risk, acquires and protects intellectual property, and so forth.

Good to Know

The multi-business corporation originated with Alfred Sloan at General Motors, who operated each of the car lines—Chevrolet, Buick, Oldsmobile, Pontiac, and Cadillac—as separate and relatively autonomous divisions within the GM corporate structure. Starting in the 1920s, Sloan spun an elaborate web of governance mechanisms, including policy and operating committees, intended to encourage divisional autonomy while empowering the corporate center to oversee the divisions in order to strengthen the overall corporation.

Good to Know

In Europe, the corporate entity is typically referred to as the Group.

If a business is part of a multi-business corporation, a question needs to be answered: what is the benefit? What is the advantage to the Olive Garden, for example, of being part of Darden rather than a separate corporation? To put this in economic language, we can look at market capitalization. It is the corporation, not the business units, that issues stock. Investors buy stock in Darden Restaurants, not in Olive Garden or Capital Grille. So, analysts can compare the corporation's market capitalization—the total dollar value of the corporation's outstanding common stock—to the apparent breakup value of the individual businesses. That apparent breakup value is an informed estimate: What value would each of the businesses within the multi-business corporation fetch on the open market if sold separately? Now, the calculation becomes straightforward. If the market capitalization is significantly higher than the apparent breakup value of the member businesses, then the corporation is adding value to the businesses. If the market capitalization is significantly lower than the apparent breakup value of the member businesses, then the corporation is thought to be destroying value.

Exhibit 3-1: M-Form Corporations

Multi-business Corporations	Some Member Businesses
General Electric	• GE Capital • GE Aviation • GE Healthcare
Darden Restaurants	• Olive Garden • Red Lobster • Capital Grille
Gap	• Gap • Banana Republic • Old Navy
TJX	• Marmaxx (Marshalls and T.J. Maxx) • Home Goods • Winners
Berkshire Hathaway	• Geico Insurance • Jordan's Furniture • Dairy Queen
The Disney Company	• Walt Disney Studios • Disney Media and Networks • Disney Parks and Resorts
Accor	• Motel 6 • Mercure • Sofitel

Good to Know

Most of the economic activity in the United States is conducted by what are known as C-Corporations, or C-Corps. The "C" designation is a reference to federal tax codes that enable the corporate entity to be taxed independently of its owners. Corporations may decide instead to incorporate as S-Corps with a very different tax structure: profits and losses are passed on to the shareholders. S-Corps, however, can issue only one class of stock (typically, no preferred stock) and may have no more than 100 shareholders. Unless otherwise noted, all references in this book to corporations should be understood to be C-Corps.

The goal of corporate strategy is to be on the plus side of that equation: to add value to individual businesses. The next important question is: *How do corporations add value to their individual business units?* Occasionally, corporations add value through the positive sentiments attached to their name. This is the concept of corporate branding. Consumers, for example, attach positive value to the name Disney, which in turn becomes associated with The Disney Company's many businesses: movies, retail stores, theme parks, ocean cruises, and the like. Business customers associate reliability with the IBM brand, an association that transfers to its member businesses: hardware, software, and business consulting.

Good to Know

Investors will often segment corporations based on their market capitalization value. Some common terms that are used include:
- Large-cap—corporations that are $10 billion plus in market capitalization.
- Mid-cap—market capitalization between $2 billion and $10 billion.
- Small-cap—under $2 billion in market capitalization.

These are not hard and fast definitions and can vary over time and by different users.

Good to Know

For a number of years, surveys have suggested that the most valuable corporate brands in the world are Apple, Coke, and Microsoft.

Of course, corporate branding can cut both ways. The deadly 2012 capsizing of a Costa Concordia cruise ship off the coast of Italy led to a precipitous drop in revenues for Carnival Cruises. Both are business units within Carnival Corporation and PLC, along with CUNARD, Holland America, Princess Cruises, and AIDA. When the brand appeal is diminished by actions of one of its businesses, the negative impact may be felt by others in the corporation.

Good to Know

Rather than incorporating, small businesses owners may form themselves into Limited Liability Companies (LLCs). LLCs have become increasingly popular in recent decades as a way to protect small investors from liability. For the most part, LLCs involve a single business with a small number of owners—known as "members"—and few or no employees. An individual who buys a condominium to rent out and generate some income, for example, may wish to use the LLC form. LLCs cannot issue stock and therefore have limited access to capital.

Corporate Strategy

Beyond the potential to add value through a corporate brand, corporate strategy comes with its own three questions: *what* businesses to own, *where* in the world to operate, and *how* to manage those businesses. The answers to these core questions will help determine how effective the corporation is.

What Businesses to Own

In determining what businesses to own, a corporation may seek to improve the competitive position of its businesses through an approach known as vertical integration. In 2010, for example, Apple acquired Siri, Inc., a company started three years earlier that had developed software to act as an intelligent personal assistant. Siri itself used voice recognition technology invented by another company, Nuance. Apple then integrated Siri into its next-generation iPhone. The goal of backward integration is to reduce costs and increase control over suppliers. Before its purchase by Apple, Siri had initiated plans to make its software available for Blackberry and Android phones. Those plans were scrubbed following the Apple acquisition.

Corporations may also engage in forward integration. In this strategy, corporations take control over the distribution of products made by their businesses. In 2009, PepsiCo announced a forward integration move (soon followed by Coca-Cola): buying its formerly independent bottlers and distributors. That is an example of forward integration through acquisition: PepsiCo bought the existing bottling companies that were involved in distributing its product. Corporations can also start their own businesses—as Apple did when it started Apple Retail as the retail outlet for its products—to gain greater control over and reap the profits from the distribution phase of a supply chain.

Corporations have another option in considering what businesses to own; this relates to diversification. Remember the requirement stated in Chapter 1: think like an investor. Like any investor, corporations can decide to diversify their portfolio of holdings by moving beyond their original business. Here, there are two options: related and unrelated diversification.

Related diversification involves moving into other businesses in the same industry. Referring back to Exhibit 3-1, you will notice a number of corporations that have followed a strategy of related diversification: Darden Restaurants, Gap, TJX, Disney, and Accor. Darden, for example, diversified beyond its original Red Lobster to operate both Olive Garden and The Capital Grille. Those chains may seem quite different, but they are nonetheless related in the sense that they are full-service restaurants. In proclaiming itself to be "the world's largest full-service restaurant company," Darden is making a statement as much about what businesses it will not own—no fast-food burger chains, for example—as what businesses it seeks to be in.

An advantage of owning businesses in related industries is that expertise, experience, and knowledge can be transferred from one business to the other within the same corporation. The Disney Company, which operates businesses related to its corporate mission of providing "unparalleled entertainment experiences based on the rich legacy of quality, creative content, and exceptional storytelling," regularly exploits opportunities for cross-marketing and selling. Popular movies morph into merchandise, theme park rides, and live entertainment.

Related diversification also allows corporations to target different customer segments within the same broad marketplace. Gap Inc., for example, sells to lower (Old Navy), middle (Gap), and higher (Banana Republic) income groups through three separate divisions. Accor operates hotel chains for the lower (Motel 6), middle (Mercure), and upper (Sofitel) price-range customer.

Corporations may use related diversification to seek opportunities to exploit synergies—that is, the opportunity for mutual benefit—that exists among businesses. That synergistic approach has the corporate center working with divisions to find such mutually beneficial opportunities. Disney, as we have seen, identifies opportunities for cross-selling among its movies, theme parks, and merchandising. Gap Inc. finds a synergistic opportunity in the purchase of raw materials for its member businesses. Accor hosts regular "innovation fairs" to spread new ideas and approaches across its many hotel chains. TJX gains economies of scale by centralizing the credit and billing activities of all its businesses in a single corporate function.

The TJX example points to one of the most common forms of synergy: shared services. In that case, corporations look for support services that are common across multiple businesses. The corporation then establishes an internal business unit—say purchasing, billing, or information technology—to provide those services to its member businesses. The hope is that the service can be provided more economically and effectively if it is centralized. In some corporations, the divisions must buy services (through transfer pricing mechanics) from these shared services centers. In other corporations, divisions can shop around for the most attractive provider. There are instances where the internal service unit becomes so effective that it sells its services outside the corporation, thus becoming a revenue generator of its own.

Despite the obvious advantages of related diversification, there are some risks. When high oil prices damage the automobile industry, General Motors has no place to hide. A decline in travel will negatively impact all of the hotel chains that operate within Accor's corporate umbrella. For these corporations, all of their related businesses can come under attack at exactly the same time.

Some corporations prefer to decide which businesses to own based not on the industry but on the relative risks and opportunities in multiple industries. These firms—in Exhibit 3-1, they would be General Electric and Berkshire Hathaway—engage in unrelated diversification. By treating businesses as an investment, unrelated diversification seeks to create a balanced portfolio.

The Boston Consulting Group Matrix (see Exhibit 3-2) is one tool corporate executives use to balance and restructure their portfolio of businesses to maximize return on shareholder investment. What is each business's potential to generate cash and offer future growth? Which businesses should the corporation be investing in and which should it simply "milk" for the last remaining revenues?

Good to Know

The label "cash cow" is applied to a business within a corporate portfolio that no longer merits much investment due to limited growth opportunities but can still generate revenues for some time and thus be "milked."

Under an unrelated diversification strategy, the corporation makes investment bets by owning businesses in multiple industries. General Electric, for example, does not rely entirely on any one industry or marketplace, but rather diversifies broadly from light bulbs and financing to aviation and health care.

Exhibit 3-2: The Boston Consulting Group Matrix

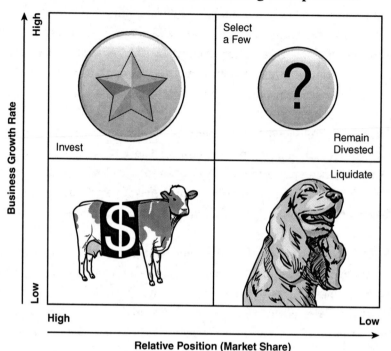

Where in the World to Operate

Corporations decide to own businesses outside their home country for a number of reasons. Foreign markets give businesses access to a broader customer base than they can find at home. Particularly when a domestic market has become saturated with competitors, the real potential for growth can come from expanding globally. Once a company decides to sell its products overseas, there will be opportunities to open support activities overseas as well—sales offices, research and development centers, perhaps even manufacturing operations—in order to be closer to the customer. Closeness offers the chance to learn more about customer needs; that fact helps explain why Brazilian-based Embraer moved its market research unit to the United States, the location of many of its most prominent customers for its regional aircraft. Moving operations to countries with a large market can also reduce transaction costs associated with moving material around the world.

Corporations move overseas to be closer to resources as well. Sometimes those resources are natural: high-quality aluminum in Australia, iron ore in Brazil, salt in Madagascar, natural gas in Russia, and so forth. The resources may be human as well: low-cost labor in Bangladesh and English-fluent, technology-savvy employees in India, for example. Companies even open operations in high-labor-cost areas—Sweden's Ericsson, for instance, situated offices in Silicon Valley—to be near sources of highly trained labor.

Because service businesses do not have a product to export, they often engage in a licensing/franchising strategy for entering a foreign market. Businesses based in a foreign country buy a license to use a trademark (typically through a royalty based on sales volume) or sign a franchise agreement. Licensing and franchising have the advantage of partnering with local owner-operators that can add both expertise and capital.

Neither licensing nor franchising requires a direct capital investment by the corporation in its overseas expansion. Many corporations prefer to engage in foreign direct investment (FDI) as a way of gaining greater control over the non-domestic operations. These corporations often engage in a joint venture with a local company. Xerox and Renault, for example, both chose to enter the Japanese market by creating a joint venture with a Japanese company: Xerox with Fuji and Renault with Nissan. In joint ventures, a third corporate entity is created that sits above the two businesses.

Point of Order

The term "joint venture" carries a different meaning for lawyers and managers. In legal terms, a joint venture is seen to be either a single or a short-lived agreement between two or more parties to engage in an activity and share the resulting profits or losses. For managers, joint ventures are typically far more formal and long-lasting.

Maximum control comes when a corporation creates a subsidiary, either by acquiring a local company or building a new business from scratch. Starbucks, for example, entered the UK by purchasing Seattle Coffee's UK subsidiary and rebranding the stores. IKEA's entry into the U.S. market came by opening new operations rather than purchasing and then converting existing ones. A corporation may expand globally by purchasing a minority position in a foreign company as Walgreens did by acquiring a 45 percent stake in Alliance Boots, the corporate owner of the Boots UK chain. A minority position typically does not qualify as a subsidiary. It can—and in the case of Walgreens's 45 percent ownership position certainly did—confer effective control.[1] The various modes of entry into foreign markets are summarized in Exhibit 3-3.

Exhibit 3-3: Mode of Foreign Entry

Mode	Description	Example
Export	Products exported overseas from a centralized production facility	Weyerhaeuser exports pulp and paper around the world
Joint venture	Two corporations from different countries join to form third entity	Renault-Nissan Alliance
Licensing/ franchising	Corporations license trademarks or sell franchises to local businesses in other countries	McDonald's expansion into India
Subsidiary	Buy existing company or start new business	Starbucks in the UK (buy existing company); IKEA in the United States (start new)
Equity position	Buy an interest in an overseas company less than 50 percent	Walgreens and Alliance Boots

How to Manage the Businesses

The third question of corporate strategy relates to *how;* that is, how will the corporate center manage its constituent businesses? As organizations grow and become more complex, they adopt a divisional structure. These divisions are the units in the corporation that enact the *who/what/how* business strategy discussed in Chapter 2. Divisional structure can take one of three forms:

1. A *product division structure* divides up units according to the products they are responsible for. Retailer TJX, for example, has numerous product divisions, including Marmaxx (a combination of Marshalls and T.J. Maxx), Home Goods, and Winners.

---

1.   The statutes and court rulings on the precise definition of "subsidiary" and "control" differ from state to state and country to country.

2. A *customer-based division structure* creates divisions that focus on different segments of the corporation's customer base. Microsoft, for example, has created one division ("Microsoft Business Division") focused on the needs of the business customer, and another ("Entertainment and Devices Division") focused on gamers and other casual though profitable customers.

3. A *geographic division structure* divides up units according to the regions of the world in which they operate. McDonald's non-U.S. operations are subdivided into four regions: Asia/Pacific/Middle East/ Africa, Canada, Europe, and Latin America. McDonald's makes this distinction based on the assumption that important differences exist in these multiple regions—in customer tastes and expectations, in supplier relationships, in governmental regulations, and in financial and labor markets—that require a differentiated response.

These are not "pure" forms, and many corporations have a combination of two if not three. Microsoft, for instance, maintains several customer-based divisions that exist alongside its product divisions: Windows Division and Online Services Division. Each business is responsible for enacting its own business strategy that is developed in consultation with the corporate center.

Good to Know

Don't confuse "brand" with division. TJX, for instance operates two different store brands—T.J. Maxx and Marshalls—under a single division: Marmaxx.

In discussing the multi-business corporation, the terms "division" and "subsidiary" are often used interchangeably. They are not interchangeable. Although both refer to business units within a corporation, there are important differences in structure. Both operate as profit centers; that is, profit-and-loss is calculated for the unit. However, a division is fully integrated into the corporation and has no legal standing on its own. A subsidiary, on the other hand, is operated as a separate business and is typically part of the corporation as the result of an acquisition. The corporation controls the subsidiary through its stock ownership (see Chapter 9 for a discussion of acquisitions), yet the subsidiary maintains independence in terms of taxation and reporting requirements. The accounts of the subsidiary are rolled up into the consolidated financial statements of the corporation based on complex GAAP rules. The subsidiary retains the ability to raise capital on its own through what is called segmental financing. More typically, the subsidiary derives capital from the corporation.

Not all acquisitions lead to the formation of a subsidiary. The acquired company may be folded into an already existing division and thus lose any independent identity. TJX, for instance, purchased Marshalls and folded two of its retail brands—Marshalls and T.J. Maxx—into a single division: Marmaxx.

An important advantage of keeping a business unit as a subsidiary operation rather than a division is that the corporation will, in some cases, be shielded from actions taken by or against the subsidiary: bankruptcy, legal actions, tax claims, and so forth. However, when the corporation can be shown to control the subsidiary, the courts may allow plaintiffs to pierce the corporate veil. In that case, the controlling entity will be held responsible for the liabilities of subsidiaries. With any attempt to pierce the corporate veil, the courts will ask the question: is the subsidiary a truly independent entity?

Corporate Structure and the "C-Suite"

All corporations, regardless of how they are structured, need some centralized functions that serve corporate interests. For that reason, the corporate center typically includes the chief executive officer (CEO) and the executive heads of corporate functions such as finance, human resources, marketing, and legal counsel. The chief financial officer (CFO), the chief marketing officer (CMO), the chief people officer (CPO), the chief information officer (CIO), the general counsel (GC), and so forth sit atop these functional units and constitute the so-called C-Suite. There may also be a chief operating officer (COO) who oversees the operating divisions of the corporation and reports directly to the CEO. The CEO also reports to the board, and members of the C-Suite may sit on the board as inside directors. I will deal more specifically with the board and its relationship to the CEO in Chapter 6.

Some of the corporate functions represented in the C-Suite may be duplicated within the divisions: finance, human resources, and marketing, for example. A division-based head of marketing will be focused mainly on the product-service offers of that division, while the CMO will seek to present a common corporate-wide image and offer resources and expertise to the divisions.[2] In that case, what often happens is the creation of a so-called dotted-line relationship. Thus, the head of marketing for product division A will report directly to the head of division A, which shows up on the organizational chart as a solid-line relationship. At the same time, the head of marketing will need to stay in close touch with and be responsive to the corporate CMO. That relationship will show up on the organizational chart as a dotted line: the relationship is there, it is important, but it is significantly less direct than the solid-line relationship with the head of the division.

Corporate Sustainability Strategies

Sustainability has become an increasingly important strategic topic to corporate executives and board members. Corporations are becoming committed to meeting the needs not only of their shareholders but also their host communities and the larger global community. Executives are looking at the processes their businesses use to develop, manufacture, distribute, and perhaps even recycle their own products. They are seeking to develop products and services in ways that are compatible with what is being called "sustainability." Some companies—Patagonia, Ben & Jerry's, Newman's Own, and The Body Shop among them—were founded on positive values concerning the social responsibility of business and the need to be a steward of a just and healthy planet. Company founders embedded values of social responsibility into the company's culture. Others—Nike and Interface Global among them—have undergone experiences that led executives to embrace going green as part of their ongoing business strategies.[3]

Sustainability matters to all citizens, of course. Corporate executives, however, find themselves in a particular situation. They are expected to take care of investments that shareholders make in their corporations. And the question arises: are shareholder expectations compatible or at odds with the demands of sustainability? To put it another way: what is the business case for sustainability?

---

2. There will be an additional discussion of the CMO's role in Chapter 5.
3. I use the terms "sustainability" and "going green" interchangeably.

Ray Anderson, the late founder and CEO of Interface Global, the world's leading manufacturer of industrial carpet, became one of the business community's leading advocates for going green. To him, the jobs of a business executive and a global citizen were completely compatible. In discussing his company's leading-edge approach to environmental responsibility, he noted:

> Costs are down, so it's saving money. Products are better, which means the top line is better. People are motivated and galvanized, which means employee morale and engagement is up. And the goodwill of the marketplace is astonishing. I don't know what else provides this kind of business case: costs are down, products are better, people are motivated, and customers are receptive—and we're winning market share.[4]

Any notion that companies need to make a trade-off between financial and environmental performance was simply a false choice, insisted Anderson. There is no trade-off.

Good to Know

Pressure for corporations to look at their impact on the environment can be traced to 1984, when an India-based subsidiary of Union Carbide experienced an environmental, social, and economic disaster. A chemical leak from its plant in Bhopal resulted in thousands of deaths and the devastation of a community. What was widely considered to be the worst industrial catastrophe in history sparked a succession of international organizations—led by the United Nations—to look at an appropriate balance between the economic requirement for development and growth, societal needs for human dignity and rights, and environmental needs for sustainability. Quickly, the role of business institutions attracted attention both as contributors to the "problem" (placing financial returns above concerns for people and the planet) and for their potential to lead the way to a solution.

The Business Case for Sustainability. Sustainability may be good for the planet, but is it good for the corporation? The board of directors has

---

4. Quoted in Jennifer Robinson, "The Business of Sustainability," *Gallup Management Journal Online* (October 3, 2009).

fiduciary responsibility, after all, to act on behalf of the best interests of the corporation. Does that responsibility leave room for going green?

Advocates of sustainability as a business imperative often use the term "triple bottom line" (sometime referred to as "people/planet/profits") in which social, ecological, and economic dimensions are all taken into *equal* account. The idea of the triple bottom line is that corporations do not have to choose among these outcomes. It is a win-win-win in which each of the three—people, planet, profits—can gain by working together.

Surveys indicate that the leading performance benefit that executives expect from going green relates to an improved company/brand image, with cost savings, competitive advantage, employee satisfaction, and innovation as other perceived benefits. Interface's Ray Anderson was especially adamant on the degree to which sustainability efforts offer "an incredible fountainhead of inspiration," frequently leading to new products and new internal processes. Exhibit 3-4 summarizes the main performance advantages of a sustainability strategy.

Exhibit 3-4: Performance Advantages of Going Green

Advantage gained:	By, for example:
Lowered cost of operating	Elimination of waste
Reduced exposure to risk	Inoculating the corporation against some future lawsuits
Increased innovation	Impetus for new products/services
Improved recruitment	Enhanced image as a "green company" makes it more attractive to potential employees
Enhanced employee motivation	Creates a sense of excitement and purpose for employees
Market differentiation	Appealing to sustainability-conscious consumers

Measuring Green Performance. Green metrics—specific objective measurements of social and environmental impact—can be built into the scorecards by which managers are measured. The choice of outcomes to be measured will be based on the company's strategy, its industry, and its social environment. Carpet manufacturer Interface, for example, measures cumulative avoided costs from waste elimination activities, degree of

Point of Order

It can and has been argued that sustainability efforts are at odds with the board's fiduciary responsibility to act in the best interests of the corporation. The courts have recognized, however, that corporations may discharge social as well as private responsibilities and still serve the long-run interest of the corporation and its shareholders.

total energy consumption required to manufacture carpet, and percentage of total energy consumption from renewable sources among its sustainability metrics.

Given the increasing public interest in sustainability, it is not surprising that a number of external organizations have devised rankings of corporations' social and environmental impact. The Dow Jones Sustainability Index, the FTSE4Good Index, and *Newsweek* magazine all offer ratings that are available to companies and the public. The ratings are not without problems, however. There can be significant differences across rating systems as to the criteria used and the relative weight assigned to each criterion. Additionally, they often rely on data supplied by the companies themselves.

Finally—Why Corporate Strategy Matters

The goal of business is to create competitive advantage. The goal of the corporation is to govern the business enterprise while managing shareholder investment and maintaining compliance with multiple federal and state statutes. The corporation attracts capital, which is then allocated to the businesses. The businesses use that capital to generate revenue that is then returned to the corporation. As attorneys add their legal counsel to corporate-level transactions, it is important to appreciate the corporation itself: What it is and what it does.

Committing the corporation to a strategy of doing well *and* doing good requires concerted and thoughtful effort. Executives will need to take on an active leadership role: articulating a vision, aligning process and metrics, coordinating with suppliers, and perhaps above all else persevering. There is no magic formula, no single tool that will quickly and easily take businesses down the path to sustainability. Legal counsel will be needed to ensure compliance with the increasingly complex web of rules and regulations that businesses need to follow. Beyond compliance, executives may also seek to position themselves and their activities in a way that allows the business to function as a steward of a just and healthy planet.

Back of the Envelope Notes

Corporations need to add value to the operations of the different businesses; otherwise, businesses should be operating on their own.

....

Three elements of corporate strategy:
1. *What* businesses to own.
2. *Where* in the world to operate.
3. *How* to manage its businesses.

....

A corporate integration strategy involves decisions concerning what businesses in the supply chain to own. There are two types of integration:
- Backward—buying or starting up businesses in the supply chain of existing corporation businesses.
- Forward—buying or starting up businesses that can act as distributors and/or sellers of the output of existing corporation businesses.

....

A corporate diversification strategy involves decisions concerning whether to own businesses in its current industry or move to a different industry. There are two types of diversification:
- Related—own multiple businesses in the same industry, typically targeting different market segments.
- Unrelated—own businesses in different industries.

....

Why globalize?
- Expand beyond domestic market, especially when growth in domestic market is slowing.
- Seek resources, both natural and human.

....

There are two types of reporting relationships depicted on organizational charts:
- Solid line—a direct reporting relationship between two individuals.
- Dotted line—an indirect reporting relationship between two individuals that requires that the subordinate stay in touch with and be responsive to the superior.

•••••••••••••••••••••••••••

The "C-Suite" refers to the chief executive officer and his/her direct reports.

•••••••••••••••••••••••••••

Advocates of the triple bottom line believe that organizations can pursue people, planet, and profits in a way that is mutually beneficial to each.

CHAPTER 4

HUMAN RESOURCE MANAGEMENT

Discussions of human resource management—the management of people in organizations—often focus on matters of legal compliance. These are the types of issues—regulations relating to equitable treatment, health and safety, wages and benefits, employee rights to privacy, drug testing, and so forth—that are most likely to be on the plate of in-house and outside counsel who work with corporations in the people management arena. Legal compliance issues are vital, of course. The issues discussed in this chapter, however, focus on the underlying rationale for a company's human resource policies and practices.

Human Resource Management

All businesses face the challenge of attracting, motivating, compensating, developing, promoting, and occasionally removing employees. Of course, all of these activities must be approached with a watchful eye on legal requirements. The goal of human resource management (HRM), however, is broader than compliance. The main purpose is to manage people in a way that maximizes performance and advances the company's strategic goals.

The chapter will focus on two areas of HRM activity:

1. Employee flow—the movement of people into, through, and out of the company.

2. Employee compensation—the design of pay systems intended to recognize and motivate employee effort.[1]

The cumulative impact of HRM decisions is intended to positively impact the nature of the relationship between the corporation and employees—the human resources—in order to enhance performance.

Employee Flow

Employee flow focuses on the need to move employees into, through, and out of the company. The goal of this HRM policy area is to ensure that the business has the "right" employees in the right jobs to do what needs to be done to achieve success. In his analysis of "great" companies, Jim Collins noted the centrality of employee flow. Get the right people on the bus, he said, and the wrong people off the bus. That's a concept and a phrase that many businesses have embraced. It's terse and direct, and it states the core challenge. Accomplishing it, however, is complex.

Good to Know

This is a good point to issue a caution about reading popular business books. Collins's "great" companies in his 2001 book, *Good to Great: Why Some Companies Make the Leap and Others Don't,* included Fannie Mae and Circuit City. Fannie Mae came close to collapsing before it was bailed out by the U.S. Treasury in 2008; a year later, Circuit City closed its doors. Their reasons for failure are varied, and the reader can still find insight from Collins's book and many other management best sellers. Still, buyer—and reader—should beware.

Moving the "Right" People *into* the Business. Individuals are interested in seeking employment at particular companies for a number of reasons: money, to be sure, as well as location, opportunity for advancement, prestige,

---

1. The original elaboration of that framework can be found in Michael Beer, Bert Spector, Paul R. Lawrence, D. Quinn Mills, and Richard E. Walton, *Managing Human Assets: The Groundbreaking Harvard Business School Program* (New York: Free Press, 1984).

and others. There is also an attraction that derives from a perception of personal alignment. Potential employees may believe that the "personality" of a company—its goals, ways of working, culture, and so on—matches nicely with their own. Conversely, they may feel that there is too much of a discrepancy between them and the organization. The type of person attracted to, say, Disney as compared to IBM will likely be quite different, even when the two companies are recruiting for precisely the same skills.

"We're looking for personality," noted a recruiter for Disney World (known in Disney parlance as a "director of casting"). "We can train for skills." Undoubtedly, businesses, especially those with strong corporate cultures such as Disney, take on personalities shaped by a combination of values and goals. Individuals, of course, have their own personalities with personal values and goals. During the joining-up process, individuals tend to seek out, and companies tend to select for, a match between organizational values and individual personalities. Exhibit 4-1 contains examples of personal values that businesses might seek. Individuals differ on all of these dimensions, and companies consider which values best advance their own strategy.

Exhibit 4-1: Examples of Personal Work-Related Values

- Value individual achievement
- Prefer working in a highly structured environment
- Seek autonomy and self-direction
- Tolerate uncertainty and ambiguity
- Direct attention outwardly
- Direct attention inwardly
- Value collaboration and collective achievement
- Respect hierarchy and power distance
- Prefer work environment with little or no status differences

The idea of attracting the right employees is important to any organization. But what, exactly, is meant by the right employee? It is useful to introduce the concept of *fit*. The right employee means an employee who fits certain needs or requirements. Even that explanation does not tell us enough, because the question still remains: *what* needs or requirements?

To help clarify the choices a business faces in the selection process, let's examine two approaches to fit. The first involves fit with a specific job, and the second involves fit with the larger company culture and values.

Person-task fit is the most common approach to hiring employees. The organization has specific tasks that need to be done, so it hires individuals with the skills required for those tasks. Need an electrical engineer? Hire the most skilled electrical engineer available (keeping costs in mind, of course). Drafting for a right tackle? Focus on the available college players with the best performance statistics. To help ensure that the business hires people with the requisite skills, human resource specialists work in a structured way to define the key skills required in the performance of core tasks. Individuals are sought, and often tested, to determine their skill level. The best-qualified individuals are then selected to fill the company's job vacancies.

The second approach to selection involves **person-organization fit.** Skills cannot be ignored, of course. Unlike the person-task approach, however, person-organization fit looks beyond the specific skills demanded of a task, focusing instead on the values of an individual. Now, the business asks: how do the values of potential hires fit with the values we are trying to promote? Person-organization fit looks at the desired mindset and personality that the organization is looking for.

But just how can businesses screen for person-organization fit? Microsoft prides itself in screening potential hires for intelligence and creativity as much as—if not more than—depth of technical expertise. Even "technical" interviews for potential software developers focus more on "thought processes, problem-solving abilities, and work habits than on specific knowledge or experience." *How many times does the average person use the word "the" in a day?* an interviewer might ask. The manner in which the individual organizes his/her thought process and attacks the problem is the key, not providing any technically "right" answer. Microsoft considers creative problem solving to be a cornerstone of the company's culture and uses the screening process to find individuals who will fit with that desired culture.

Recruitment interviews like those used by Microsoft are one technique that organizations can use to screen for the right employee. Personality tests, behavioral interviews, and role-playing

Point of Order

Employees have a loyalty duty to their employers, typically interpreted to require that they avoid acting in ways that compete with the employer's interests.

activities are other approaches. Of course, not *all* issues of person-organization fit can be resolved in the selection process. Training can help by reinforcing fit, while removing employees may occasionally be required. Still, getting it as right as possible in the selection phase certainly will reduce both the cost and time associated with training and minimize the difficulties—both emotional and financial—associated with removal and replacement.

Moving the "Right" People *through* the Business. Employee development refers to explicit HRM initiatives undertaken by the business to help employees develop new skills. Those skills can be classified as either technical or general. Technical skills involve the particular chores required of the employee's job. Just as lawyers need technical skills to draft required documents or file contracts, other employees need to learn how to operate certain technology, how to file reports, and how to negotiate with suppliers. General skills involve tools that help an individual manage and motivate employees, plan for future performance, coordinate with peers, and resolve conflicts. Businesses will often offer training sessions, require certificate training, and support education for their employees to build both technical and general skills.

Despite all the benefit that can be derived from attending training sessions, the most powerful form of employee development occurs through on-the-job learning. Providing employees with a variety of experiences creates an opportunity for individuals to gain guidance and feedback. From the company's perspective, on-the-job learning also offers an opportunity to evaluate employee potential. How well does an employee do when faced with a new and challenging situation?

A key to such on-the-job learning is the provision of regular, ongoing, and honest assessment and feedback. Employees need to know: Am I living up to expectations? What new experiences should I be seeking? How is my contribution to the performance of the company being perceived by others? Performance feedback is used to evaluate performance and help determine salary and/or bonuses. Feedback also serves a vital role for the employees and the organization in terms of ensuring ongoing fit.

Most employees want to be contributing members to a successful business. Companies have an interest in ensuring that they are maintaining an inventory of required skills and competencies. One of the most important opportunities for developing required skills and competencies among employees arises from a well-run performance appraisal system.

Although corporations implement performance appraisals quite differently, some generalizations can be made. Performance appraisals tend to:

- Be regularly scheduled events, occurring annually, semiannually, or even quarterly.

- Be individual, one-on-one sessions between a supervisor and a subordinate.

- Be guided by a form designed by the corporation's human resource department.

- Involve some sort of grading system, covering both specific performance elements and an overall evaluation of effectiveness.

Performance appraisals benefit the business by improving the performance of individual employees. The process can identify poor performers and future leaders. It can also help identify the gap between the skills the organization currently possesses and the skills it needs. From the data generated by the performance evaluation process, businesses can construct developmental tools—training, career pathing, mentoring, and so forth—as well as guide future recruitment and selection.

Performance appraisal can occur at all levels of a business. Companies often use the appraisal process to identify individuals with the potential to assume, in time, top executive roles. A process known as succession planning is then put into place in order to manage the development of those skills. In succession planning, top executives regularly review all managers at or above a certain hierarchical level, looking at both performance and potential, and devise developmental plans for their most promising individuals.

Moving the "Wrong" Employees *Out* of the Business. Remember Collins's statement about the importance of getting the right people on the bus? He also talked about getting the "wrong" people off the bus. He was not talking about downsizing or any other large-scale workforce reduction intended to cut costs rapidly. He was instead referring to removal and replacement. Downsizing typically involves large-scale layoffs. Removal and replacement, on the other hand, is a more specific, targeted intervention. The goal of removal and replacement is to deal with individuals who cannot or will not develop required skills and competencies.

Good to Know

Large-scale layoffs occur when corporations close down a division or plant or make general reductions in their workforce to cut labor costs. In such cases, employers are obliged to adhere to statutes relating to discrimination as well as the procedures set out in their employee handbook concerning issues such as severance pay and pay for unused vacations. However, most employee handbooks also contain a clause allowing the corporation to change the rules. Also, severance pay is typically not a secured fund, so the corporation may not be able to meet its goal of paying severance.

Removal and replacement becomes more salient when a company is changing its strategy. New skills and competencies will be required. Companies that move from traditional retailing to e-commerce might find that some of their current employees are either unwilling or unable to acquire the required new skills.

Point of Order

Most employment in the United States is based on the doctrine of at-will employment. Unless otherwise specified in the employment contract, both the employer and the employee may terminate the relationship with no liability. Statutes exist, however, to enumerate "improper grounds" for termination, including discrimination against a protected group.

Compensation Policies

Compensation represents one of the strongest, and perhaps most immediate, HRM policies designed to promote performance and support strategy. Companies expend a huge amount of resources on pay—time, energy, and money (anywhere from 40 to 70 percent of sales revenues). Compensation takes two forms: *salary* and *bonuses*. Salary is the guaranteed annual income associated with a job, with the guarantee contingent on the fulfillment of the employment contract. A bonus is a payment above and beyond salary based on some measure of performance. Even though many employees receive both a salary and a bonus, each should be considered separately.

Salary. Let's talk first about how firms set employee salaries. It is important to understand that salary is associated mainly with a job rather than an individual. Depending on the position an employee holds, he or she is placed within a salary range, often referred to as a grade. The employee can move up within the grade range based on some combination of performance and seniority. A promotion moves an employee to a higher pay grade. Just how businesses determine the amounts attached to each grade is a complex process, but one that rests on an assessment of the contribution each job makes to the overall business: the greater the contribution, the higher the amount of money attached to the range.

Businesses will also conduct salary surveys to determine how much employees are paid in similar positions in other companies. Private consulting firms and trade associations can provide that comparative data. Knowing what competitors pay allows a business to make a choice: should we match competitors' pay ranges, exceed them, or position ourselves below them? Pegging salaries above competitors' allows a business to attract an ample supply of talented job seekers. On the other hand, a business may peg salaries *at* or even *below* the market. The goal here is to save money on compensation while using other factors—the image of the company, the desirability of the region in which the company operates, and/or the generosity of non-pay benefits—to attract desirable job applicants. Hourly pay is similar in that it consists of a contracted, preset amount.

Good to Know

Corporations may impose a uniform job classification system and salary range on all divisions, or they may allow divisions the autonomy to devise their own salary plans.

Bonus. Bonuses do not alter base salary. An employee may receive a bonus one year, but substandard performance the following year, either by the employee or the business, can reduce or eliminate the bonus. Bonuses may be eliminated altogether by companies seeking to reduce costs. For that reason, bonuses are often referred to as *variable,* or *at-risk,* pay.

Point of Order

It is useful here to distinguish between exempt and nonexempt employees. The 1938 Fair Labor Standards Act (FLSA) required that nonexempt employees—mainly non-supervisory personnel—be paid on an hourly basis for overtime work. FLSA also carried provisions for a federal minimum wage.

Good to Know

Salaries and bonuses are operating expenses that must be reported on a corporation's income statement and subtracted from revenues to help determine net income. But what about stock options? Do they need to be considered as an expense? The answer from the Financial Accounting Standards Board is unequivocal: yes. This was not always clear. However, in 2004 the FASB issued a statement requiring that all stock options be reported as an expense based on the fair value of the stock at the time of its "measurement date": the date on which both the number of options an individual employee is to receive and the exercise price of the options are known. The exercise price is the price at which the option may be purchased. The difference between the employee's exercise price and the fair value of the stock on the measurement date is considered the expense of the option to the company. SEC investigations were occasionally triggered when companies "backdated" the option grant to reflect a lower value for the stock. Currently, however, the SEC requires the reporting of all option grants within two days of their issue. That rule, combined with a clearer understanding of the expensing requirement, has significantly decreased the number of legal actions associated with stock option reporting and dating.

Stock options are a form of reward intended to align the interests of executives with the interests of stockholders. Favorable tax laws have made these plans more popular in the United States than elsewhere, although a number of multinational firms—PepsiCo, Bristol-Myers Squibb, DuPont, and Merck among them—have offered stock options to virtually all of their employees worldwide. Most companies select a mix of performance pay rather than rely on any one approach.

Finally—Why Human Resources Matter

Legal actions often arise out of a company's HRM policies and practices. Are employees being treated and compensated fairly and in accordance with prevailing laws? Are the firm's hiring, promotion, and firing practices in compliance? These legal questions occur within a much broader context. In their management of people, companies are intending to meet both their strategic and financial goals. The ability to place legal actions within a larger business dialogue requires a familiarity with the more strategic elements of human resource management.

Back of the Envelope Notes

Two key policy areas in human resource management:
1. Employee flow—movement of people into, through, and out of the company.
2. Employee compensation—design of compensation systems.

••••••••••••••••••••••

The goal of employee flow policies is to ensure that the business has the "right" employees in the right jobs to do what needs to be done to achieve success.

••••••••••••••••••••••

Attracting the "right" people to come work for an organization is as much about looking for individuals whose values fit with the culture of the company as screening for technical skills.

•••••••••••••••••••••••

Think of employee skills as having two dimensions:
1. Technical skills—know-how to perform specific tasks.
2. General skills—ability to manage, motivate, plan, coordinate, resolve conflicts, etc.

•••••••••••••••••••••••

The most powerful learning occurs not in training sessions but in actually doing the job and receiving feedback on performance.

•••••••••••••••••••••••

The pay grade into which an employee is placed—based on an assessment of the job's contribution to the business—determines the upper and lower ends of that employee's salary range.

•••••••••••••••••••••••

A bonus is considered a form of variable, or at-risk, pay because a payout occurs only if a predetermined level of performance is reached.

•••••••••••••••••••••••

The Fair Labor Standards Act requires that nonexempt employees—mainly non-supervisory personnel—be paid on an hourly basis for overtime work. Exempt workers are paid on salary, and the employer is not required to pay for overtime work.

•••••••••••••••••••••••

Stock options are an expense that must be reported on a corporation's income statement.

Chapter 5

MARKETING

"The purpose of business," wrote management guru Peter Drucker, "is to create and keep a customer." Marketing involves the set of activities that seeks to analyze the marketplace, identify and attract potential customers, and design the optimum approach to monetizing the interaction between the customer and the company. Although often thought of in terms of "selling" or "advertising," marketing embraces a far broader set of activities. Researching the marketplace, segmenting potential customers, determining the best conditions under which to sell a company's products, pricing, and maintaining customer relationships—all within the framework of a business's strategy—are core to marketing.

At the same time, a company's approach to marketing raises a number of significant legal issues. Developing new products for the marketplace requires attention to intellectual property protections, while the new products themselves raise issues of quality and liability. Particularly in this Internet age, market research finds itself in the middle of an ongoing tug-of-war between consumers' desire to maintain control over personal information and marketers' desire to exploit personal data for commercial purposes. Pricing and promotion decisions raise their own concerns ranging from price fixing to deceptive advertising. By understanding the overall functionality of marketing in a business context, legal advisors can help focus activities and enhance a business's capacity to implement its market strategy effectively.

Core Marketing Activities

Marketing focuses attention on the interaction between the business and its customers—both current and potential future customers. Although much of marketing takes place in a specialized functional area, the entire organization is focused on creating value for the customer. Marketing is largely a business-level function in that it supports a business's who/what/how strategy. Multi-business corporations often maintain a corporate marketing function headed by the chief marketing officer (CMO) that can support business-level activities, lead initiatives that impact multiple divisions, and promote the corporate brand.

Marketing is prominent in consumer goods industries (electronics and restaurants, for example, referred to as B2C businesses). Many B2B businesses (businesses for which the main customer is another business) either downplay or ignore marketing as a separate activity. That contrast between B2C and B2B marketing can be seen within General Electric.

GE allows its separate divisions to decide whether to create a marketing function. Some B2C businesses did: GE Appliances and NBC Universal, for example.[1] B2B businesses, including GE Aviation, avoided creating a marketing function altogether, relying instead on the quality of their products and personal relationships with a few key customers in the industry to fuel revenue.

In 2003, CEO Jeffrey Immelt altered the corporate strategy, seeking to find growth from within: GE-developed products and technology. To help shepherd that internal growth (referred to as "organic growth"), he created a corporate marketing department and added a chief marketing office to the GE C-Suite. That office became the "torchbearer" for internal innovation. Corporate marketing first initiated Imagination Breakthroughs, a portfolio of growth projects across the many GE business units, and then Ecoimagination, a corporate initiative to develop clean technologies.

When it comes to customer focus, B2B businesses face a special challenge not typical of the B2C world. Identifying the end user of consumer

---

1. NBC-Universal Media is now a separate company owned jointly by Comcast and GE.

goods in B2C businesses such as electronics and automobiles is relatively straightforward. For B2B marketing, however, targeting the customer is a more complex affair. In a business, the end user and the buyer of a product or service are typically different. That does not change the usefulness of companies engaging in marketing activities between the customers and the business, but it does add a layer of complexity.

Identifying the Target Market

In Chapter 2, I discussed the three questions for which every business must provide a strategic answer: *Who* is our target market? *What* is our product/service? *How* will we deliver our *what* to our *who* in such a way as to generate profit? Marketing touches on all three elements of strategy, starting with the identification of a target market. The specialized process of market research—conducted by internal experts, external consultants, or some combination—provides the company with the intelligence (both raw data and analysis) to make sense of the *who* question.

In particular, market research can help identify various segments of the buying population in order to answer three questions:

1. What segment(s) should be included in our target market?
2. What are the attributes of that/those segment(s) that will impact their perception of our product?
3. How do we deliver a product to meet the needs of that target market?

The process is built on the concept of market segmentation.

Marketers segment customers by placing them into homogeneous groups. There are many lenses that can be applied to accomplish segmentation, demographics—age, sex, income, and so forth—being the most obvious. Geography, individual psychology, even how consumers behave when they shop are also considered.

An increasingly popular tool for segmentation involves lifestyle segmentation: grouping customers based on three dimensions (the AIO Dimensions):

- Activities (work, shopping, hobbies, sports, social events)
- Interests (food, fashion, family, recreation)
- Opinions (about themselves, social issues, business, products)

The idea of market segmentation is the more a business knows about and understands its customers, the better able it is to serve them. Market researchers typically conduct interviews and surveys, use focus groups, mine data on online shopping behavior, and even track volunteer customers' brain activity when they shop.

There is a wealth of data on individuals available for collection and analysis; some accessible for free and some through private providers. Marketers do not look at one factor in arriving at their analysis but rather take into account multiple variables. That technique, known as multivariate analysis (MVA), involves observation and analysis of more than one statistical variable at a time in order to understand the multiple dimensions that impact consumer behavior.

Good to Know

The U.S. government provides a wealth of free online demographic data. The Small Business Administration (SBA) maintains a data and statistics site. The U.S. Census Bureau offers multiple data access tools including The American Fact Finder. FedStats.gov provides access to official government-collected statistics. In addition, the SBA provides an online tutorial for conducting market research.

In collecting data on consumers, businesses need to be aware of both privacy and public relations issues. In its required 2011 10-K filing,[2] Google listed as one of the risks facing the company "improper disclosure of personal data [which] could result in liability and harm our reputation." As Google executives are well aware, the Internet provides a virtually endless source of data on individuals that can be mined by companies. The availability of data also raises important privacy and legal concerns. Those concerns kick in most particularly when children are involved. The Children's Online Privacy Protection Act (COPPA) of 1998 mandates that website and online service operators acquire verifiable parental consent before they use, collect, or disclose any personal information about children under 13. The Federal Trade Commission (FTC), which administers the law, recently extended the protection to apply to third-party data brokers such as Twitter and Facebook, a category that did not exist when the original statute was passed.

---

2. Required 10-K filings will be discussed in Chapter 7.

Market research can also identify underserved customer segments. The decisions by Progressive Insurance to target motorcycle owners and by the United Services Automobile Association to focus on armed services personnel, both current and retired, and their families reflected the market insight of these two companies of the special connection they could make with these underserved segments of the insurance industry. Of course, any choice of target market must take into account the potential for both reaching these groups and generating profits from the resulting revenues.

Good to Know

To be clear, a company can define its target customer market broadly and still be successful. Certainly, Amazon does—and is. In these cases, however, the company needs to look at other elements of its strategy in order to stand out from its competitors. In the case of Amazon, what differentiates that company from other online retailers—in fact, from other retailers generally—is extraordinarily high levels of customer service.

Good to Know

B2B businesses also segment their customers, choosing to focus on types of businesses (e.g., small, large), industries (e.g., health care providers, government), location of businesses (e.g., North America, Pacific Rim), or some combination.

Good to Know

The hugely popular management book *Blue Ocean Strategy* urged companies to pay attention to non-customers as a way of differentiating themselves from competitors.[3] Just to cite two examples from the book: Cirque du Soleil targeted individuals who avoided traditional circuses (often because they objected to the use of live animals). And Australia's Yellow Tail wine made a highly successful entry into the U.S. market by focusing on non-wine drinkers, particularly beer drinkers who were put off by the complexity of purchasing wine.

Building Relationships

Traditional marketing focused on making a sale to a customer; that is, on the transaction between the seller and the buyer. More recently, relationship marketing has moved beyond the transaction to attend to building

---

3. W. Chan Kim and Renee Mauborgne, *Blue Ocean Strategy: How to Create Uncontested Market Space and Make Competition Irrelevant* (Boston: Harvard Business School Press, 2005).

a long-term relationship with a customer. Many businesses have adopted customer relationship management (CRM) systems and processes for measuring customer habits and behaviors with the goal of increasing customer loyalty. The efforts range from loyalty programs to after-sales service in order to maintain the relationship.

The premise of relationship marketing is that return customers are more profitable than new customers. Both acquiring a new customer and retaining a current one involve costs to the company. However, the acquisition costs—advertising, discount coupons, special offers to first-time customers, and so forth—are thought to be significantly higher than the cost of retention. Thus, each dollar spent by an existing customer generates more return on a firm's bottom line than does the same dollar spent by a new customer. Additionally, customer spending tends to increase over time as he/she returns to a business for additional purchases. And by creating highly satisfied customers, companies find their marketing efforts become more effective: personal referrals often prove more attractive than do advertisements and other promotions.

Not all returning customers are equally desirable. Businesses will occasionally divest themselves of unprofitable customers, either individually or in segments. Professional sports teams have been known to ban individuals from buying tickets, while some casinos bar addicted gamblers. In 2007 Sprint Nextel informed 1,000 individuals who were considered high maintenance end-users that they would no longer be customers. More typically, companies do not disclose that they are "firing" customers. However, when customer demands are persistently driving up costs, businesses occasionally consider this approach.

Reaching a Target Market with the 4 P's

It would be a virtual impossibility to engage in a sustained discussion about how marketing helps businesses reach out to their target customers without eventually encountering the 4 P's, a classification system devised by E. Jerome McCarthy. Reaching a target market requires careful consideration of four elements:

1. Product—the offer the company is making to the customer.
2. Price—the terms set for the exchange between the buyer and seller, usually but not always stated in monetary terms.

3. Place (or distribution)—the process by which the product gets to the end-purchasers.

4. Promotion—the methods used for building awareness and acceptance of a product or brand.

The 4 P's—illustrated in Exhibit 5-1—capture the main activities of marketers.

Product. The product is the most tangible element of the 4 P's. Still, defining the product is more complex than simply pointing to a tangible object. Starbucks, for instance, sells more than cups of coffee. CEO Howard Schultz talks about Starbucks offering customers a "Third Place"—not home, not the office—to relax, chat, and meet. No one will rush you out the door. There will be comfortable chairs, free Wi-Fi, and lots of electric outlets to plug in laptops. All of that is part of the $5 or more a customer pays for a latte. And Starbucks is not alone in selling intangibles along with its tangible product: McDonald's sells consistency and convenience, IBM sells reliability, and Apple sells pizzazz.

In fact, most products have both tangible and intangible attributes. The tangible attributes are physical and relate to the functionality of the product. Intangible attributes are psychological and evoke emotional responses

Exhibit 5-1: The 4 P's

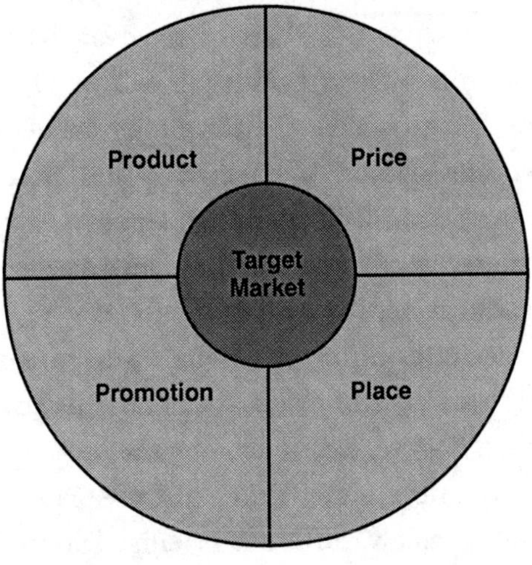

from users: satisfaction, a sense of belonging, pride, status, and so forth. When Porsche introduced its new SUV, the Cayenne, to the German market, executives made a decision to relocate vehicle assembly from Finland (where the Boxster was assembled) to Germany. Porsche's management believed that despite the increase in costs attached to assembling in Germany, customers would be willing to pay more for the intangible element of the Cayenne: "Made in Germany."

Good to Know

Commodities are one class of products that have no intangible attributes. Wheat is wheat, coal is coal. There have been some successful attempts to differentiate products that were at one point considered commodities: chicken in grocery stores, for example. Businesses that sell commodities can either follow a low-cost strategy or differentiate themselves with service.

Point of Order

The principle of product liability is that the seller or maker of a product is liable to compensate a user for injury due to defects in design, production, or marketing of that product. If the manufacturer can be shown to have been negligent by failing to exercise reasonable care, the plaintiff can rely on the *res ipsa loquitur* doctrine.

The attributes of the product—both tangible and intangible—are designed to appeal to the needs and wants of the business's intended market segment. Companies may, of course, wish to appeal to multiple customer segments with differentiated offers. As we saw in Chapter 3, corporations often set up separate divisions to deal with different market segments. The Gap has different divisions—Gap, Old Navy, and Banana Republic—to address the needs of different types of shoppers. Accor has different hotel chains—Motel 6, Mercure, and Sofitel—to attract different customer segments. Dell operates separate divisions for different segments: consumers, small and medium businesses, large enterprises, government, and education.

Other businesses offer different product lines aimed at different market segments within a single division. Retail chains regularly differentiate stores—an A store, a B store, and so on—by the segment represented in the store's immediate vicinity: same chain, just a somewhat different mix of products, and, quite possibly, different pricing. Different lines can also be incorporated into a store mix as a way of attracting a new segment. Coach introduced a new line of women's accessories—the Poppy line—designed to attract a younger shopper than its more traditional demographic. Poppy line items were displayed in the same stores as the traditional line, standing out with a distinctive style and a lower price point.

Price. Decisions on how to price a business's product or service are among the most important and complex of the 4 P's. Pricing decisions are related to a firm's revenue model, the manner by which exchanges with customers are monetized. For examples of different revenue models, we can look at the online world. Does the company generate revenue through subscription (Netflix), advertising (Google, Facebook), or a combination of the two (Pandora Internet Radio)?

Before considering how to price an offer, executives need to consider the company's revenue model. For an example of a pricing strategy based on an understanding of the revenue model, look at Green Mountain Coffee. Its revenue model emphasizes profitable revenue generated by its K-Cups and not the delivery system: the Keurig coffee brewer, which the company also sells. Pricing of the coffee brewer reflects the revenue model. The goal in pricing the Keurig brewer was not to maximize return on the machine but rather to build market share and demand for the more profitable K-cups. Once a customer purchases a Keurig brewing machine, he/she is locked into the purchase of Green Mountain Coffee's patented K-cups.[4]

Ultimately, customers determine price through their willingness to pay. The concept of customer value suggests that no product or service has any intrinsic value: there is no value unless and until a customer is willing to pay for the item. That may be true in the long run, but in the short run, businesses must devise strategies for placing a price on an item. That challenge is especially important when the product or service is new to the market.

For any new product, companies will perform a break-even analysis, which identifies the point at which different prices of a product will meet the total costs of producing and delivering that product and deliver desired

---

4. Lock-in disappears once the patents expire and competitors enter the market.

margins at various sales volumes. Now the strategic decision becomes: do we set the initial price high or low? High initial pricing, known as skimming, is intended to attract a small, select group of consumers who will build and, it is hoped, spread enthusiasm. Low initial pricing, known as penetration, is intended to attract a large customer base and build market share as a way of warding off potential competitors.

Value pricing—starting pricing decisions by understanding how much value a customer will attach to the product—represents the most common approach to making pricing decisions. In some industries, however, the seller and the buyer agree to use cost-plus pricing. This approach—which begins with the cost of producing and delivering a product or service and then adds the desired profit margin to determine price—is more likely to occur in B2B businesses, especially government contracting. Law firms might also use cost-plus pricing to replace hourly billing with an agreement between the firm and the client on a fixed price for a transaction based on the estimated number of hours plus an agreed-upon profit for the firm.

Point of Order

In the mid-1990s, a price fixing charge against Archer Daniels Midland led to both high fines and prison sentences. Marketing practices can have legal, even criminal implications. Food and drug and antitrust statutes carry criminal charges, and price fixing can be classified as a felony.

An increasingly popular approach to pricing is to separate the price for shopping from the price for buying. Think, for example, of the popular global home furnishing chain, IKEA. One of the ways that IKEA maintains low prices on its products is by raising the price of shopping. As any customer of IKEA knows, the price for shopping is high, not so much in dollars but in effort: pulling items off the shelves, packing them in your car, driving them home yourself, and then assembling. Those are all activities that a traditional home furnishing retailer performs for the customer, bundling the costs into the price of the item. The IKEA customer is apparently willing to trade off the high price of shopping for the low price of buying.[5] Companies often unbundle the various prices involved in consuming to allow customers to exert some control over the price of buying.

---

5. IKEA customers have the option of subcontracting home delivery and assembly, thus lowering the price of shopping but raising the price of buying.

Place. In marketing parlance, "place" is both a noun and a verb. As a noun, place refers to the locale—either physical or virtual—where the customer encounters the product. As a verb, "to place" means to distribute and sell and involves the chain of companies (known as the channel) that delivers a product to its end purchaser. Some businesses offer a direct channel between themselves and the end purchaser: you can buy your Dell computer directly from the company.[6] Apple supplemented online sales with its own retail business to provide a place for customers to "meet" the product.

Place is also a noun, referring to the physical location where end purchasers "meet" a product and make the buy/don't buy decision. Placing a product in the wrong setting can be a near-death experience for retailers. Take, for example, Lacoste. The high-end French-based sportswear company

Point of Order

Pricing decisions are rife with legal implications. Certain pricing practices raise red flags from a legal perspective:

- Vertical price fixing (also known as resale price maintenance, or RPM)—deals with attempts by a manufacturer to enforce a minimum selling price on its products or prevent discounting by the retailer. Suggesting a selling price (manufacturer's suggested retail price, or MSRP) does not constitute vertical price fixing.
- Horizontal price fixing—deals with agreements between two or more competitors to set a minimum price on an item.
- Price discrimination—deals with a manufacturer charging different retailers different prices for products (does not apply to services).
- Predatory pricing—deals with the practice of charging a low price in order to drive out competition and then raising prices.

These practices run afoul of various federal antitrust laws, as well as many state fair trade laws, if and when the impact is anti-competitive.

---

6. Dell also sells its product through other retail stores such as Staples and third-party solutions providers.

entered the U.S. market through a licensing arrangement with an American company, Izod. That agreement allowed Izod to carry the prestigious Lacoste trademark—a green crocodile—on its clothing. The partnership worked well for several decades. However, as demand declined for the "preppy" style, Izod began selling its green crocodile sportswear in down-market retailers and discount outlets. Lacoste executives feared that these places sent the wrong message to customers: Lacoste wanted its products to be placed in luxury surroundings. To help reposition the brand, Lacoste severed ties with Izod and altered the place in which Lacoste clothing was sold, eliminating discounters in favor of stand-alone boutiques in prestigious shopping areas and high-end retailers.[7] Place matters.

Promotion. Promotion—the steps taken to increase awareness, acceptance, and consumption of a product or brand—is perhaps the most commonly thought-of aspect of marketing. Businesses need to let customers know not only what products they are selling but how and why the product

will create value for them. Promotion may focus on a brand name rather than an individual product—fast-fashion giant Zara, for instance, advertises its name and overall appeal and image rather than individual items of clothing. Disney, IBM, and GE are other corporations that believe in corporate brand promotion.

Promotion is about more than advertising, however. The goal is to create a hierarchy of effects. Awareness of a new product is the first stage,

---

7. After being purchased by PVH Corporation, Izod went through its own transformation to be positioned (without the green crocodile, of course) as a moderate-price clothing line.

one that requires building consumer interest in learning about the product. That awareness needs to include not just the fact that the product exists but an understanding of the value proposition of the product: why would I as a consumer be better served with this product than with a competing one? Getting a customer to try a product once is a start; getting the customer to make repeated purchases, however, is the ultimate victory for promotional efforts.

There are legal ramifications that marketers need to be sensitive to as they mount a promotional campaign. Companies routinely engage in "puffing" a product: making vague but extravagant claims. Coke, for instance, has over the years claimed:

- Ice cold sunshine.
- America's favorite moment.
- Things go better with Coke.
- It's the real thing.
- Can't beat the feeling.

Are those claims true, or even provable? They are not really meant to be. The FTC's position on puffery is that consumers are well aware that the claims are not to be taken literally.

More serious, specific distortions can lead to scrutiny from the FTC and significant penalties. There are some industries for which other government watchdogs will scrutinize promotional claims especially closely. The U.S. Food and Drug Administration (FDA), for example, exercises oversight over the promotional efforts of pharmaceutical companies. In 2009 the FDA required Bayer Pharmaceuticals to sponsor a campaign correcting previous advertising that overstated the benefits and understated the risks of its popular birth

Point of Order

The marketing of pharmaceuticals requires special attention. Drugs are approved by the FDA for a specific "indication" or purpose. Any attempt by a company to promote a drug for a non-approved purpose—referred to as an off-label use—violates FDA regulations and can result in serious penalties. Of course, drugs approved for one condition may also be effective at treating other ailments. For example, a beta-blocker, originally approved for treatment of high blood pressure, was soon found to be effective against angina and heart attacks. Although pharmaceutical companies are prohibited from marketing their drugs' off-label uses, doctors are free to rely on their own medical expertise to prescribe drugs for off-label purposes. Pharmaceutical companies may share published articles about off-label uses with physicians in response to an "unsolicited request" for such information. Because the line between appropriate and illegal promotion is often a fine one, and recent financial penalties have been extremely large, legal advice on drug marketing is practically required.

control pill, Yaz. Promotions aimed at children are looked at closely by the Children's Advertising Review Unit, an industry self-regulatory review body.

The Power of the Internet

The Internet has proven to be a powerful tool for businesses seeking to gain data on and communicate with customers. Some companies—McDonald's, Apple, and MasterCard, among them—have used the Web to generate customer-produced ads. Procter and Gamble (P&G) has been a corporate pioneer in the use of social media to build a customer bond. P&G sites like Beinggirl.com and the blog site Pampers Village allow customers and the company to communicate in an unfiltered way and build communities of end users. However, as P&G found out, the Internet can be a double-edged sword.

When P&G introduced Dry Max technology into its Pampers diapers, a mother launched a campaign on her Facebook page claiming the new technology caused diaper rash. Soon, 7,000 parents joined in the complaint about Dry Max, leading the U.S. Consumer Product Safety Commission (CPSC) to launch an investigation. P&G conducted its own counteroffensive, using social media to respond to concerns by providing scientific evidence that contradicted the claim while offering advice to parents. Eventually, the CPSC stood by P&G's technology and the product remained on the market. And P&G remained committed to employing the Internet as an important marketing tool.

It has always been risky to disappoint customers. Companies that consistently over-claim and under-deliver will pay a price in customer backlash. But now, thanks to the power of the Internet, a single unhappy customer can exert unprecedented power. Sites such as ihatestarbucks.com or allstate insurancesucks.com can convert individual complaints against a company into larger customer movements. Occasionally, companies respond with the threat of lawsuits. Those threats, however, can lead to a negative public reaction while bringing even greater attention to the initial complaint.

Finally—Why Marketing Matters

"No customers, no business," as the saying goes. Identifying the desired target market for a company's products and services is a key strategic question. Market research is invaluable in identifying those target groups and understanding what they are looking for and willing to pay for the company's offer. Other marketing activities help promote and price products and place them in a way that is most appealing to those customers. Marketing specialists within the business are responsible for implementing effective research and promotional programs. But the responsibility of delivering value to customers is part of the task of every member of the company.

Legal counsel, both in-house and outside, have a vital role to play as well. No business is well served when marketing efforts create legal problems. As we have seen, most of the legal implications of marketing—pricing, promoting, managing the sales channel, and so forth—require expert analysis and advice. This is a case where in-house and outside counsel, functional specialists, and general managers can all benefit from a collaborative partnership.

Back of the Envelope Notes

By selecting a desired target market, businesses can shape their product/service offers to meet the specific needs of that market. Businesses that seek to have a broad, general market appeal will try to differentiate themselves from competitors by other aspects of their operations—for instance, service or price.

. . . .

Contemporary marketing tends to focus more on building long-term relationships between the business and its customers than on simply making a sale.

. . . .

Return customers are often more profitable to a business than are new customers.

. . . .

For strategic and profitability reasons, not all customers or customer groups are equally desirable. Therefore, businesses occasionally divest themselves of customers.

. . . .

The 4 P's of marketing:
1. Product
2. Price
3. Place (distribution)
4. Promotion

•••••••••••••••••••••••

Products have tangible and intangible attributes:
- Tangible—physical product, functionality, etc.
- Intangible—satisfaction, sense of belonging, prestige, etc.

Customers will pay for both *if* they are perceived as adding value.

•••••••••••••••••••••••

A revenue model specifies how exchanges with customers will be monetized. Even within the same industry, competitors may have different revenue models.

•••••••••••••••••••••••

In a competitive market, price is ultimately determined by the customer's willingness to pay. Nonetheless, companies must have a pricing strategy to help them position the product.

•••••••••••••••••••••••

Two strategic approaches to pricing:
1. Value pricing—set price based on value of the product/service to the end user.
2. Cost-plus pricing—set price based on the cost of producing and delivering the product/service plus a desired profit margin.

•••••••••••••••••••••••

Sales channel refers to the firms that move a product from the producer to the end user. Some companies may engage in direct sales to end users, but most go through distributors, third-party sellers, and retailers. Many companies use a combination of sales channels.

•••••••••••••••••••••••

In the retail world, the setting in which a good is sold to the end purchaser can be an important intangible aspect of the product's value.

•••••••••••••••••••••••

The five elements of a company's promotional mix are:
- Advertising—paid presentations and promotions in which the sponsoring product/brand is identified.
- Sales promotion—short-term incentives designed to encourage potential consumers to try out the product/service.
- Personal selling—representations made by the company's sales force to make sales and build relationships.
- Public relations—general promotion of the brand as well as handling of negative stories, reviews, and events.
- Direct marketing—connecting directly with targeted individuals to make sales and build relationships.

....

Promotion aims to achieve a hierarchy of effects:
- Awareness of a new product.
- Interest in learning about the new product.
- Evaluation of the important attributes of the product.
- Trial through first purchase.
- Adoption by repeated purchases based on experience in trial.

CHAPTER 6

CORPORATE GOVERNANCE

Perhaps no issue relating to the world of business has attracted more attention in recent years than that of corporate governance. Broadly speaking, corporate governance refers to the framework employed by a corporation—as established in its charter through the articles of incorporation—to ensure that the business is being run effectively and in a way that advances the interests of the shareholders who have invested their capital. The board of directors—the group that sits at the intersection of shareholders and executives—shares the fiduciary responsibility with top executives to act in the best interests of the corporation. It must perform its duties in compliance with prevailing laws and regulations.

Governance matters are rich in legal implications. In-house and outside counsels play a vital, complex role in ensuring good governance and adequate compliance. Recent federal legislation recognizes and codifies the relationship between legal counsel and compliance, thus increasing the significance of understanding the dynamics of governance. But governance is about more than compliance; it is about the proper management of the corporation's affairs.

At the Center of Corporate Governance: The Board of Directors

The board of directors is the group of individuals that oversees the operations of the corporation. Members are elected by and act on behalf of shareholders. The vast majority of directors on boards are current or former corporate executives. Many directors possess a financial background. Given the heavily regulated environment of corporate governance, it is not surprising that lawyers are being increasingly recruited to serve on boards. It is vital at the outset to understand a key distinction among board members: the distinction between inside and independent directors.

Inside and Independent Directors

Until recently, the majority of board members were executives from the company itself: the CEO, the CFO, and other top executives. With the passage of the Sarbanes-Oxley Act (SOX) in 2002, the power balance shifted from inside directors to independents. By law, all public companies—defined as companies that sell stock shares to the public—must now have a majority of directors who are independent. Key board committees—the audit and compensation committees—must now be composed entirely of independent directors. Additionally, the law requires that independent directors meet regularly in independent-only sessions.

Good to Know

Not all public companies sell their stock on a formal exchange such as the New York Stock Exchange or NASDAQ. A company may also sell stock over-the-counter, thus avoiding the regulations imposed by the particular exchanges. However, most large companies prefer listing on an exchange because of the prestige and access to capital that comes from such a listing.

Good to Know

Privately held companies, including those owned by private equity firms, are exempt from the disclosure laws and regulations imposed on public companies. Investors in private firms are expected to protect their own interests.

To be classified as independent, a director cannot be a current corporate executive. The definition of independence as promulgated by various stock exchanges goes beyond that simple statement. The individual cannot have been employed by the company recently—say, a CEO staying on the board after retiring or leaving the company. There are also restrictions on the dealings an individual may have either personally or professionally with the company that figure into definitions of independence.

Good to Know

Just to clear up a common misunderstanding, the terms "non-executive" director and "independent" director are often used interchangeably. They are not interchangeable. "Non-executive" means that the individual is not currently an executive of the company. All independent directors are also non-executive. However, a just-retired CEO who remains on the board would be a non-executive director but *not* an independent director.

It can sometimes be unclear where to draw the line on the true independence of an independent director. In 2004 RiskMetrics, a leading risk management and governance consulting firm, challenged the independence of a director on Coca-Cola's board. That director, whom the board classified as independent, was Warren Buffett, founder and CEO of Berkshire Hathaway. RiskMetrics noted that Berkshire Hathaway had made a huge investment, then valued at $10 billion, in Coke. Additionally, a Berkshire subsidiary, Dairy Queen, was a Coke customer. Buffett received strong support from the Coke board, which noted, "Mr. Buffett's independence is consistent with the standards set by the New York Stock Exchange." Buffett stayed on the board. Nonetheless, in a highly interdependent world, independence is a concept that will be tested from time to time.

Point of Order

Fiduciary responsibility to act in the best interests of the corporation applies to members of the board, but not to individual shareholders, who are entitled to act in their own interests. When a shareholder is elected to the board, fiduciary responsibility to the corporation as a whole takes over. A complication occurs when a shareholder who is not a director nonetheless accumulates a controlling interest in the corporation. If such a shareholder can control the makeup of the board with his/her voting power, then the requirement for fiduciary responsibility on behalf of the corporation is likely to be in effect.

Board Responsibilities

Regardless of the classification, all board members share a single and fundamental responsibility. As established by state law, directors have a fiduciary responsibility to act in the best interests of the corporation. Two of the fifty states add "and its shareholders" to that formulation. Even without that added statement, it is understood that shareholders are owners of the corporation and elect board members to act on behalf of the corporation's best interests. None of the state laws is specific as to how to define or measure "best interests."

In addition to that fiduciary responsibility, board members have a loyalty duty to avoid divided loyalties when they are acting as board members, a care duty to stay informed and make deliberate and carefully considered decisions, and a supervision duty to make sure that corporate executives are complying with relevant laws and regulations. In carrying out these duties, board members are allowed—indeed expected—to exercise business judgment in carrying out their responsibilities. They may, for example, take action to enact the social responsibilities of the company to its host community as well as broader social and environmental interests. Even if those considerations do not increase return on investment for shareholders in the short term, boards can pursue the corporation's social responsibilities. However, because corporate interests are paramount—that's the point of fiduciary responsibility—the board must not act in a way that is detrimental to those interests.

These duties are not expected to place board members inside the daily working of the organization. Quite the

Point of Order

The only circumstance in which directors are required by state law to maximize the corporation's current stock price is when the company is "deemed for sale"; that is, the sale or breakup of the corporation is thought to be inevitable. The so-called Revlon doctrine established by the Delaware Supreme Court and followed by numerous other states requires that the directors, in this situation only, narrow their focus to maximize *immediate* shareholder value.

Point of Order

A director's care duty—the obligation not to be negligent—is taken in the context of business judgment. Directors have leeway here to exercise business judgment. Even if a judgment call turns out poorly for the corporation, the courts typically assume that the directors used their best business judgment. Legal actions relating to care duty typically occur in conjunction with claims of self-dealing and/or conflicts of interest.

Point of Order

Shareholders may sue boards for breach of responsibility. "Direct" litigation involves an action taken in the name of the shareholders for an injury to those shareholders' interests caused by the board. "Derivative" litigation takes action on behalf of the corporation itself, alleging that the board has injured the corporate entity.

opposite. Boards give executives the autonomy required to run the business, acting rather as advisors and overseers. Exhibit 6-1 summarizes the key jobs of a corporate board as well as the areas in which it needs to be well informed.

Exhibit 6-1: What Boards Do[1]

Need to Do:	Need to Know:
Approve strategy decisions made by executives	Corporation's competitive position and key customers
Approve major financial decisions	Corporation's current financial status
Select, evaluate, and compensate CEO	Performance and capabilities of CEO and top executives
Oversee succession planning for CEO replacement	State of the larger managerial talent pool in the corporation
Ensure legal and financial compliance	Where the corporation stands on legal and compliance matters

Good to Know

Individuals or institutions that hold large blocks of stock in a company may seek to place a representative on the board. That is perfectly legitimate, even common. However, once that individual is elected to the board, he/she is required to represent the overall interests of the corporation.

How the Board Works

Board members are nominated by the board itself, usually through its nomination or governance committee, and elected by shareholders at the annual shareholders' meeting. The typical board is composed of between 8 and 16 members who may be elected for either a one-year term or for staggered three-year terms. Most corporations follow a one-share/one-vote rule, although a number have opted for separating their common stock into two or more classes. In that arrangement, known as dual-class shares, some favored classes of common shares are awarded more than one vote per share, perhaps as many as 30. These favored shares are not available to the public and are typically held by founders and their families, company executives, and

---

1. Based on Jay W. Lorsch and Robert C. Clark, "Leading from the Boardroom," *Harvard Business Review* 87 (April 2008), p. 112.

allies of the incumbent executives and board members. The effect of dual-class shares is to give insiders greater leverage over board member selection.

Good to Know

Some boards have adopted a staggered term approach in which only a minority of directors stand for re-election at any one time. This approach is thought to make it difficult for a group of investors to wrest control away from the board.

Much of the board's work is conducted through committees as established in the articles of incorporation. Many boards will select a small group of members to serve as an *executive committee.* When quick action is needed and it is impossible to gather a quorum of the entire board, the executive committee can be authorized to meet and take action. All public companies must have an *audit committee.* This is the group that oversees financial reporting and hires an independent auditor to ensure the rigor and integrity of those reports. The SEC requires that all members of the audit committee be independent and financially literate (that is, able to read and understand a financial report), and that at least one member be a financial expert with experience as an accountant or in some related aspect of financial management.

In addition to the audit committee, boards are required to organize a *compensation committee,* also composed exclusively of independent directors. Often working with external compensation-focused consultants, this committee designs and administers the compensation package for the CEO and other top executives. The *nominating committee,* sometimes referred to as the *governance committee,* identifies potential new board members and also ensures that plans are in place for CEO succession. Finally, a *corporate secretary*—often the general counsel—oversees communications among directors and between directors, senior management, and shareholders; keeps all corporate records (including board meeting minutes); and ensures that directors have the necessary information to carry out their duties.

Good to Know

A shareholder has the right to inspect corporate books. That right, however, is limited to good-faith efforts made for proper purposes at the appropriate time and place with the goal of enhancing the interests of the corporation and shareholders.

Boards are run by the chairman of the board. In the United States, it is common that the CEO also serve as the chairman. The overlap in those two roles has led to considerable discussion and analysis. Some argue that having the same person serve as both CEO and chairman can undermine the independence of the board, while others suggest that unless the two are unified, employees will be uncertain as to exactly who is leading the corporation. In Europe, most corporations split the two positions, and in the United States, companies that received relief under the 2008 Troubled Asset Relief Program (TARP) were required to split the roles.

Boards are required to hold at least one meeting a year that is exclusively for independent directors. In fact, boards will frequently hold executive sessions for independent directors immediately following each full board meeting during the year. The independent directors analyze the performance of the CEO, debate any major differences with company strategy, and discuss the performance of the overall board. When the CEO is also chairman, the independent directors need to designate a lead director to oversee their meetings.

Board Meeting Schedules. Each board meeting is convened around a particular topic. The "four seasons" of board meetings might follow this pattern:

- Winter meeting—setting and reviewing compensation for top executives and board members.
- Spring meeting—planning for management succession, including an assessment of available talent.
- Summer meeting—evaluating the strategic plan.
- Fall meeting—reviewing the budget.

There are additional topics that may also require a meeting:

- Major transactions, including mergers and acquisitions.
- Financing corporate operations.
- Significant management changes.
- Major litigation, investigations, and other crises.

Prior to all meetings, management creates a "board book" that serves as the informational lifeblood of the meeting. Required background material, financial performance updates, subcommittee materials (for example, the compensation committee's report for the winter compensation meeting), and specific proposals that require a vote are delivered in a timely manner to directors who are expected to exercise their care duty by preparing for the upcoming session.

Good to Know

Like the rest of the world, boards are increasingly availing themselves of digital data opportunities. A number of commercial portals exist to give board members secure digital access to board books. These sites also offer capabilities for secure online conferences.

Point of Order

Shareholders are entitled to vote by proxy; that is, they may authorize an agent to vote on their behalf.

Say on Pay. As noted above, setting and administering executive pay is one of the core tasks of the board of directors. In recent years, it has become one of the most controversial tasks as well. Board members seek to establish a compensation package that allows the corporation to attract and retain top-quality executives. Shareholders and government regulators have expressed concern about what is perceived to be the rising compensation packages awarded to CEOs, while questioning the degree to which that compensation is tied to corporate performance.

The matter of executive compensation has been attracting attention for decades. In 1992, the SEC added the Executive Compensation Disclosure Exchange Act that required firms to disclose their rationale for executive compensation and its relationship to performance. Additionally, compensation in excess of $1 million would not qualify as a deductible expense for tax purposes unless that compensation was tied to performance. Following passage of SOX, the SEC adopted the Compensation and Disclosure Analysis (C&DA) rule requiring that corporations provide disclosure and explanation of compensation paid to directors, the CEO, the CFO, and their three other highest paid executives. That report includes the overall objectives of the executive compensation plan and must detail and justify each element of the plan.

Scrutiny of executive compensation continued with the Dodd-Frank Wall Street Reform and Consumer Protection Act of 2010. Public companies are now required to allow shareholders to participate in an advisory vote on the executive compensation plans adopted by the board. Despite the existence of some pressure to make these votes binding, the current Say on Pay rule only establishes a non-binding advisory vote to be held at least every three years.

Finally—Why Corporate Governance Matters

Because the corporation's articles of incorporation amount to a binding contract, the governance framework must be followed in order to ensure compliance. But let's be honest. Good corporate governance does not generate revenues. It does not find new customers, develop new products, or build market share. So, other than as a compliance obligation, what makes corporate governance so important?

To start with, corporations rely on the willingness of the capital markets to invest the capital that fuels development and growth. That decision to invest is ultimately based on trust. Investors want to know how well run the corporate enterprise is: Are the mechanisms in place to ensure that directors and executives are meeting the legal obligations as well as their fiduciary responsibilities? Is good care taken to avoid conflicts of interest or other activities that may hurt the corporation and damage the interests of shareholders? Serious attention to corporate governance is required to build a lasting, positive relationship with the various players in the capital markets.

Then there is the matter of performance. Although it is true that corporate governance does not generate revenue, it does bring stability, order, and clarity of purpose to what is often a sprawling, complex organization. Confusion can undermine mindful strategy execution, sending mixed and uncertain messages to managers. In-house and outside counsel can help ensure corporate governance focuses energy and action in a clear strategic direction. That is the value of good corporate governance.

Back of the Envelope Notes

Board duties:
- Fiduciary duty—look after the interests of the corporation.
- Loyalty duty—avoid divided loyalties while serving on board.
- Care duty—stay informed, make deliberate, carefully considered decisions.
- Supervision duty—make sure executives are complying with relevant laws/regulations.

······················

Board duties are not expected to place board directors directly into the operations of the business. Boards give executives the autonomy required to run the business and act as advisors and overseers.

······················

Board structure:
- Executive Committee—subgroup authorized to make quick decisions.
- Audit Committee—oversees all financial reporting (all independent directors).
- Compensation Committee—designs and administers compensation for top executives (all independent directors).
- Nominating Committee—seeks nominees for open board seats and oversees planning for CEO succession.
- Corporate Secretary—oversees communications and keeps necessary records.

······················

SOX requires that independent directors meet as a group at least once a year to discuss CEO performance and other pertinent matters. The independent group is run by the designated lead director in cases where the CEO also serves as chairman of the board.

······················

The "four seasons" of board meetings include:
- Winter meeting—setting and reviewing compensation for top executives and board members.
- Spring meeting—planning for management succession, including an assessment of available talent.
- Summer meeting—evaluating the strategic plan.
- Fall meeting—reviewing the budget.

There are additional topics that may also require a meeting.

······················

"Say on Pay" involves a requirement that shareholders be allowed to take a non-binding vote on executive compensation plans put in place by the board at least every three years.

CHAPTER 7

RISK MANAGEMENT AND COMPLIANCE

Ask directors of corporate boards what keeps them up at night, and the answer typically comes down to one word: risk. Unanticipated, unknown disruptions caused by both external and internal factors: tsunamis and government actions as well as financial reporting mistakes and even fraud. Then ask a follow-up question: other than shareholder value and bottom-line performance, what should boards pay the most attention to? The answer comes back: risk management. Clearly, risk is a topic that demands consideration.

Risk management has important legal ramifications. Counsel is often involved in crafting a response when companies are forced to deal with the negative consequence of risk and noncompliance. Furthermore, general counsel is typically part of the firm's executive committee that assumes primary oversight of companywide risks. To help appreciate the challenge, this chapter will address two types of risk: decision-making risk and financial controls risk.

The Nature of Risk

Business decisions—whether to invest in a new product, move to a new overseas market, buy or sell an asset, change a supplier, and so forth—involve risk. To a greater or lesser degree, *every* decision is risky. The definition of risk is simple: the impact of uncertainty on outcomes. No significant management action has an absolutely certain outcome. For that reason, corporations must manage risk by asking a series of questions. How much risk are we willing and able to take on? What is the risk involved in different decisions? How do we respond if risky decisions turn out badly?

All corporations have both a risk capacity and a risk tolerance. Risk capacity, which is established by the board, refers to the level of risk a corporation considers itself capable of absorbing based on its available capital (cash and other highly liquid assets). With risk capacity, executives ask, in essence, if the worst-case scenario actually happens, will the company be able to absorb the loss?[1]

Risk tolerance refers to the appetite for risk within the parameters set by risk capacity. This is more a matter of attitude than liquidity. Firms that are willing to take risks up to their maximum capacity for absorbing loss are said to be risk aggressive. Not all corporations are willing to be so aggressive, however. In these instances, board members and top executives prefer to leave considerable space between their risk capacity and the risks they take. When a gap exists between risk capacity and risk tolerance, the size of that gap defines the firm's risk aversion.

Risk tolerance will vary from corporation to corporation and is influenced by numerous factors: the values and beliefs of the company's original founders and current board members, the relative volatility of the industry in which the business operates (consumer goods, for instance, tends to be a more volatile industry than public utilities), and the age and size of the business. Corporations that have made a strategic commitment to innovation will need to take on greater risk—investments in R&D, acquisitions, and so forth—than, for example, companies that are content to operate in mature markets.

---

1. As discussed in Chapter 1, the downside potential of risk will impact how much cash the cooperation will need. There is always an opportunity for tension between a risk-averse board's desire to keep a large cash reserve and shareholders' interest in investing in growth and receiving dividends.

Risk Management

"Hope for the best, plan for the worst."

There may still be some wisdom in that old adage. However, in a volatile, dynamic world—not to mention a business environment subject to increasing scrutiny and regulation—that traditional approach to risk management is far from sufficient. Investors, bond-rating agencies, and Wall Street analysts all expect businesses to manage risk in such a way that promotes shareholder value.

Every corporation carries a portfolio of risks. For multinationals, every country in which the corporation operates presents an additional set of risks. Corporate boards and CEOs, therefore, are responsible for creating a portfolio of investments and managing the resulting risks. Investors, who have their own risk capacity and tolerance, use a measure called beta to help make investment decisions. Beta (ß) is a measure of a company's stock price volatility relative to the overall market and is assumed to reflect the corporation's risk profile.

Good to Know

A beta of 1 means that the volatility of the company's stock matches the volatility of the overall market; a beta of less than 1 means the stock is less volatile than the general market; and a beta over 1 means the stock is more volatile than the overall market.

The process of managing risks follows four steps: identifying and sorting risks, assessing risks, responding to risks, and reporting risks. We can look at each one in turn.

Identifying and Sorting Risks. Risk comes in many types. Therefore, the first step of risk management is to identify and sort through the full portfolio of risks. There are many classifications that executives may use for that purpose. I will present one that sorts risks into four classifications: strategic risks, operational risks, market/credit risks, and hazards:

1. *Strategic risk* arises from decisions in which uncertainty can affect the achievement of an corporation's strategic goals. Strategic risk can arise from external uncertainties: how competitors will respond, how customers will react, and so forth. It can also arise

from decisions made within the corporation: decisions to acquire another company, to move into foreign markets, and so forth.

2. *Operational risk* arises from the management of internal processes and the uncertainty that accompanies choices made concerning supply chain partners, quality assurance programs, compliance policies, and so forth.

3. *Market/credit risk* arises from the uncertain impact of management decisions concerning extending and receiving credit (will loans be paid in full and in a timely matter?) and liquidity issues (do we have enough cash on hand to cover unexpected losses?), as well as fluctuations in foreign exchange rates that might help (or hurt) overseas sales and purchases.

4. *Hazards* are the uncertainties associated with the possibility of accidents and disasters than can arise from natural forces as well as human error.

Different corporations may use different categories. What is important is that executives reach a comprehensive understanding of the corporation's risk portfolio in order to move to the next step: risk assessment.

Good to Know

Exchange rate fluctuation is frequently noted as "FX," for foreign exchange.

Assessing Risks. Not all risks are equally deserving of attention: some have more probability of occurring (likelihood), and some contain more potential to disrupt the corporation (significance). For that reason, the next step in the risk management process is to analyze risks in terms of likelihood and significance. This is a step typically handled by specialized experts. Their approach involves the creation of a risk map on which risks are placed according to the two axes of probability and impact (see Exhibit 7-1). Such an analysis helps clarify both the need for attention and the type of attention required.

A process known as scenario planning or stress testing can be helpful in understanding and planning for high-impact events, even events like natural disasters that are difficult, if not impossible, to predict. That may seem counterintuitive: how can managers plan for unpredictable events? What they can do is look at past unpredictable events—natural and man-made

Exhibit 7-1: Risk Assessment

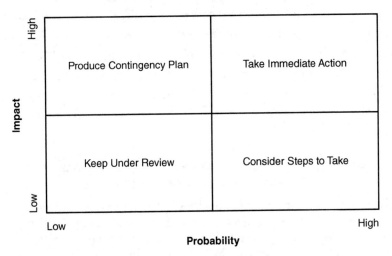

Based on John Hargreaves, "Quantitative Risk Assessment in ERM," in John Fraser and Betty J. Simkins, eds., *Enterprise Risk Management: Today's Leading Research and Best Practices for Tomorrow's Executives* (New Jersey: Wiley, 2010), pp. 219–236.

disasters, economic collapses, government overthrow—and utilize computerized models to generate what-ifs. How would these events impact the corporation in the here and now? This is a far from perfect approach, but it can give managers a sense of how well prepared the corporation is to absorb low-probability/high-impact events.

Responding to Risks. Once risks and their upside/downside potential are identified, managers can make decisions based on risk capacity and risk tolerance. What risks should be taken on? What risks need to be monitored closely? What risks are to be avoided?

Executives evaluate the risk portfolio for the entire corporation, often referred to as "enterprise risk," to help inform decisions concerning allocation of capital and approval of projects. In addition, ongoing processes for assessing risks—including a clear definition of responsibility/accountability, common frameworks and metrics across the entire corporation, and expected reporting duties (detailing who is responsible for reporting risk assessment to divisional management, to the executive committee, and to the board)—are put into place.

Reporting Risks. The SEC requires that a corporation's 10-K, as well as its quarterly 10-Q, include an assessment of risks that it faces. Exhibit 7-2 presents a summary of the risk factors presented in a recent Google 10-K filing. Notice that the risks are not placed on a risk map. The SEC does not require that analysis to be disclosed. Good risk management, however, would involve a thorough analysis of the likelihood and the potential impact of such risks, report in detail on that analysis to the board, and make plans for how to manage those risks.

Exhibit 7-2: Google Risks as Reported in Form 10-K (summarized—not complete)

- Risk from competition: "Our business is rapidly evolving and intensely competitive, and is subject to changing technology, shifting user needs, and frequent introductions of new products and services."
- Risks from internal processes, including: new product development, investments in new strategies and technologies; acquisitions that do not pay off as planned, and inability to manage rapid growth.
- Risks from external environment, including the economic environment (revenue from advertisers could decline), the regulatory environment (pressures from governments concerning privacy matters), potential attacks by hackers, inability to protect intellectual property, and chance of being sued by others.
- Risks from technology, including new technology that can block the ads that generate Google's revenue.

Good to Know

The 10-K annual report is not the same as the glossy report typically prepared in advance of the annual stockholders meeting, although most glossy reports include the 10-K.

The Special Concern about Global Risks

Firms that do business around the globe face additional risks that must be identified, assessed, and managed. Even if a corporation does not own any operations in foreign countries, it is likely to be selling products overseas as well as buying supplies from overseas supply chain partners. Think of the disruption caused by the 2011 Japanese tsunami and nuclear disaster to American auto companies as Japan-based supply chains collapsed.

The World Economic Forum suggests three categories for organizing global risks:

- *Economic* risks, including sharp changes in food and oil prices, fluctuations in the strength of the U.S. dollar in relationship to the local currency, and national fiscal crises.
- *Environmental* risks, including drought, rising sea level, water shortage, earthquakes/storms/floods, and regional health concerns.
- *Geopolitical* risks, including war, terrorism, state failure, and population migrations.

Corporations involved in any type of international business transactions with supply chain partners, distributors, subsidiaries, joint ventures, and so forth are expected to include these additional risks in their overall risk assessment.

Financial Control and Compliance

When corporations report on their performance through their annual 10-K or quarterly 10-Q, they provide shareholders with a balance sheet detailing assets and liabilities, an income statement showing revenue and expenses, and a statement of cash flows showing the company's operating and investment activities (see Chapter 1). These reports—required by the SEC for all public companies—are intended to provide investors and regulators with a clear and accurate picture of the firm's finances. The question of how to ensure that the data is, in fact, clear and accurate falls under the heading of financial controls.

As mentioned earlier, the risk associated with management decisions comes with an upside as well as a downside. That is *not* true of the risk involved in financial controls; there is no legitimate upside to risky controls. To ensure that the financial report offered by the company is clear and complete, executives must offer an assessment of the effectiveness of their financial controls. Although there is always some risk of error or misstatement, the goal of financial controls is to minimize that risk.

> **Point of Order**
>
> The 1934 Securities Exchange Act used disclosure as the main vehicle for regulating the securities market, following the principle articulated by Louis Brandeis that "sunlight is the best disinfectant."

How Effective Are a Firm's Financial Controls?

SOX Section 404 requires management to report on the effectiveness of the corporation's internal controls over financial reporting. What control mechanisms are in place and how well are these controls executed? The corporation is also required to file a report by an independent auditor that provides its own assessment of those controls. Those independent auditors must be certified by the Public Company Accounting Oversight Board (PCAOB), a nonprofit corporation created by Congress to oversee the implementation of SOX. The auditor is paid for and reports to the board's audit committee, made up exclusively of independent directors.

Good to Know

Small public companies—defined as having $75 million or less in "public float" (the value of stock owned by the public rather than by directors and executives)—are not required to use an independent auditor.

Searching for Deficiencies. The goal of internal controls over financial reporting is to reduce as far as possible the occurrence of misreporting or misstatement in the corporation's financial status. Those control mechanisms include the hiring and training of qualified staff members, checks and balances on the data entered into the reports, and senior management commitment to clear and accurate reporting. A risk assessment has to do with the effectiveness of the controls that are in place and the rigor by which those controls are enforced. Is there a risk that the report itself is flawed?

Management and the independent auditor are required to search for deficiencies or weaknesses in the company's financial controls. Deficiencies can come in many forms, including:

- Evidence that sales contracts are regularly rewritten by salespeople.
- Evidence of inadequate training.
- Evidence that financial reports are not completed in a timely and thorough manner.
- Evidence that accounts are not handled in a consistent manner across multiple operating units.
- Evidence of lack of segregation between responsibilities for approving expenditures and making purchases.

Even if those deficiencies have not actually led to any misstatements in the financial report, they must be addressed and corrected to ensure accuracy.

The system seems to rely entirely on self-reporting. Companies are expected to surface, report, and correct control deficiencies. That raises a question: Are company executives themselves capable of making an honest assessment of their own internal practices? After all, the act of reporting weaknesses is likely to undermine investor confidence and make it difficult to raise capital.

A number of controls are in place to help encourage honest reporting. First, there is the role of the independent auditors. Their reputations are on the line. Arthur Andersen, a former Big Five accounting firm, slid into bankruptcy after its questionable independence from a client—Enron—was revealed. In addition, SOX (Section 307) requires that the company's in-house attorneys report any violations of the rules of compliance. Dodd-Frank provides a provision for a whistle-blower to bring evidence of noncompliance directly to the attention of the SEC. And finally, SOX established criminal risks for CEOs and CFOs who falsely certify accounts.

Reporting on Deficiencies. The PCAOB requires the use of risk assessment tools to establish different gradations of weaknesses. The PCAOB establishes three levels of deficiencies in the financial controls of a company:

- Control deficiency—a flaw that creates a remote chance that a wrong number may appear in the financial statement.
- Significant deficiency—a more serious flaw or number of small flaws that increase the possibility that bad numbers will distort earnings.
- Material weakness—enough serious flaws that there is a more-than-remote possibility that material error will be made.

> ## Point of Order
>
> The rules adopted by the SEC to implement Section 307 of SOX in relation to the conduct of in-house attorneys include:
> - Requirement that in-house attorneys report evidence of a material violation "up the ladder" to the general counsel or CEO.
> - Requirement that in-house attorneys bring that evidence to the attention of the audit committee or the full board if the general counsel or CEO does not respond appropriately.
> - Allowance for in-house attorneys to reveal confidential information regarding their interactions in order to prevent material violations or illegal acts.

"Material errors" are not strictly defined, but typically are errors that would impact the earnings report and/or affect the stock price. The discovery of significant deficiencies needs to be reported internally as well as to the independent auditing firm. The revelation of a material weakness, as would be expected, triggers a more serious response.

Once a firm discovers a material weakness as defined by the PCAOB—remember, a weakness does not mean there *is* a mistake in the reporting, just a more-than-remote chance of a serious mistake—executives cannot sign off on their 10-K report because they cannot state that the firm's financial controls are effective. The 10-K does not have to detail the weakness, but the independent auditor will review the financial figures to find any inconsistencies. The company may issue a restated financial report and will be required to detail the changes it has made in the control systems. The most typical deficiencies that lead to restatements are problems with expense reporting and misclassification (misplacing items on balance sheets, income statements, cash flow statements, and so forth). Exhibit 7-3 contains the independent auditor's report on financial controls in place at Apple that found no material weakness.

The Governance of Risk

The chapter opened by noting the degree to which boards need to oversee and address risk. Although risk management has always been high on boards' agendas, the financial crisis of 2008–2009 led to a renewed sense of urgency, enforced by additional laws and regulations. The Emergency Economic Stabilization Act of 2008 and the Dodd-Frank Wall Street Reform

Exhibit 7-3: Apple Corporation's 10-K Filing: Report on Internal Control over Financial Reporting

By Independent Auditor

We have audited the accompanying consolidated balance sheets of Apple Inc. as of September 24, 2011 and September 25, 2010, and the related consolidated statements of operations, shareholders' equity and cash flows for each of the three years in the period ended September 24, 2011. These financial statements are the responsibility of the Company's management. Our responsibility is to express an opinion on these financial statements based on our audits.

We conducted our audits in accordance with the standards of the Public Company Accounting Oversight Board (United States). Those standards require that we plan and perform the audit to obtain reasonable assurance about whether the financial statements are free of material misstatement. An audit includes examining, on a test basis, evidence supporting the amounts and disclosures in the financial statements. An audit also includes assessing the accounting principles used and significant estimates made by management, as well as evaluating the overall financial statement presentation. We believe that our audits provide a reasonable basis for our opinion.

In our opinion, the financial statements referred to above present fairly, in all material respects, the consolidated financial position of Apple Inc. at September 24, 2011 and September 25, 2010, and the consolidated results of its operations and its cash flows for each of the three years in the period ended September 24, 2011, in conformity with U.S. generally accepted accounting principles.

We also have audited, in accordance with the standards of the Public Company Accounting Oversight Board (United States), Apple Inc.'s internal control over financial reporting as of September 24, 2011, based on criteria established in *Internal Control—Integrated Framework* issued by the Committee of Sponsoring Organizations of the Treadway Commission and our report dated October 26, 2011 expressed an unqualified opinion thereon.

/s/ Ernst & Young LLP

and Consumer Protection Act of 2010 in particular aimed to reform traditional approaches to risk management.

Boards have primary responsibility for setting risk capacity parameters and for overseeing enterprise-wide risks. The directors meet regularly with their company's chief executive officer, chief financial officer, and general counsel, as well as other senior managers, to gain a thorough picture of the corporation's operations. Exhibit 7-4 contains a statement from a recent Dell 10-K filing stating the board's risk management responsibilities.

Exhibit 7-4: Dell 10-K Statement of Board Responsibility for Risk Management

As part of its oversight responsibility, the Board is responsible for the oversight of risks facing the company and seeks to provide guidance with respect to the management and mitigation of those risks. An analysis of strategic and operational risks is presented to the Board in reports submitted by the Chief Executive Officer, the Chief Financial Officer and the General Counsel as well as by other members of Dell's senior management who regularly appear before the Board to provide detailed overviews of the businesses they oversee. In addition, at least once each year, each member of the Board meets with the management of the business segment of the director's choice to review in detail the segment's operations, customer set, strategies and risks. Directors also have complete and open access to all Dell employees and are free to, and do, communicate directly with management.

Boards also delegate risk management responsibilities to various subcommittees. The delegation of risk management employed by Dell's board, detailed in Dell's wording below, is typical.

- The Audit Committee is responsible for the oversight of risk policies and processes relating to Dell's financial statement and financial reporting processes. The Audit Committee reviews and discusses with management, the independent auditor and the Vice President of Corporate Audit significant risks and exposures to Dell and the steps management has taken or plans to take to minimize or manage such risks.

- The Financial Committee is responsible for reviewing and approving the plans and strategies with respect to corporate finance, capital transactions, and other transactions involving financial risks.

- The Leadership Development and Compensation Committee monitors the risks associated with succession planning and development as well as compensation plans, including evaluating the effect Dell's compensation plans may have on risk decisions.

- The Governance and Nominating Committee monitors the risks related to Dell's governance structure and process.

Each of the committee chairs reports to the full board at its regular meetings concerning the activities of the committee, the significant issues it has discussed, and the actions taken by the committee.

For most corporations, the day-to-day oversight of risk falls to the chief financial officer. To add greater capacity to the CFO's role, many companies have created a chief risk officer (CRO). That task involves pulling together and paying attention to all the various risk-related functions—insurance, legal, compliance, and security—in one office. Dodd-Frank also requires that financial institutions maintain a board-level risk committee, and a number of nonfinancial companies have adopted that practice as well. General Electric's risk committee, for example, states in its charter that its purpose is "to assist the board in its oversight of the company's management of key risks, including strategic and operational risks, as well as guidelines, policies, and processes for monitoring and mitigating such risks."

Finally—Why Risk Management and Compliance Matter

Laws and regulations—SOX, Dodd-Frank, and the rules of the SEC and various stock listings—help define the rules of corporate governance. Much of the impetus for the current era of regulation grew from the concern that corporate financial statements were not truly reflecting the state of the company's health, thus misleading shareholders and regulators alike. For that reason, many of the regulations take specific aim at the internal controls installed within the corporation to ensure a candid and thorough appraisal of the company's finances, thus allowing investors to make an informed choice about how to allocate capital.

Risk management is a top priority to boards and chief executives. The regulatory environment in the twenty-first century has increased the demand for and expectation of assessment, management, and disclosure of risks. The twin pressures to increase shareholder return while managing risks have become more intense than ever. With risk as a priority, in-house and outside counsel have a significant role to play in risk assessment and planning, in ensuring compliance, and in helping the company achieve an appropriate balance between the need to manage risk and the need to increase shareholder wealth.

Back of the Envelope Notes

The overall risk profile of a corporation will influence investor decisions. Some investors will tolerate greater risks in hopes of greater returns.

....

Types of risk:
- Strategic—uncertainty from decisions impacting achievement of strategic goals.
- Operational—uncertainty from decisions relating to internal processes, including supply chain choices.
- Market/credit—uncertainty from decisions concerning extending and receiving credit.
- Hazards—uncertainties from natural forces and human error.

....

Look at risk in terms of probability and impact; those with high probability and high impact should be red-flagged for immediate attention.

....

Effective risk management includes:
- Use of a common risk assessment/risk review framework.
- Executive leadership clarifying risk capacity/risk tolerance and ensuring enterprise-wide monitoring and measuring along with appropriate reporting.
- Risk awareness embedded in strategic planning, capital allocation, and other daily decisions.
- An early-warning system in place to highlight possibilities that risks will rise above capacity/tolerance thresholds.

....

Corporations operating internationally will need to pay special attention to the risks that arise within different countries and regions.

•••••••••••••••••••••••

Corporations work to minimize risk that their financial reports are inaccurate.

•••••••••••••••••••••••

Three levels of deficiencies in financial controls:

Level 1 (lowest): control deficiency—a remote chance that a wrong number may appear; should be corrected.

Level 2 (medium): significant deficiency—the possibility that bad numbers will disrupt earnings; must be reported internally as well as to independent auditing firm.

Level 3 (highest): material weakness—more-than-remote possibility that an error has occurred that can impact income statement and/or stock price; must be reported in 10-K; may lead to restated financial report along with details of changes that have been made in financial controls.

•••••••••••••••••••••••

Day-to-day oversight of risk management falls to the chief financial officer (CFO). To add greater capacity to the CFO's role, many corporations have created a chief risk officer (CRO).

CHAPTER 8

INTELLECTUAL
PROPERTY

Knowledge and ideas have increasingly replaced machines and buildings as the currency of our economy. In the United States alone, economists estimate that corporations spend over $1 trillion a year developing intellectual assets, more than is spent on the physical assets that until recently fueled commerce. As a percentage of gross national product (GNP), investment in intellectual capital has tripled, while investment in physical capital has been flat. The Internet certainly helps explain that explosion, but other factors—the increasing complexity of technology, the globalization of commerce, and the speed of innovation and change among them—contribute. Virtually any business, regardless of size, scope, or industry, traffics significantly in knowledge and ideas.

Given these developments—the growing importance of knowledge and the increasing investment in developing it—there is little surprise that the management of intellectual assets has become a major task for corporate executives. And as much as in any other area of legal practice, the oversight, protection, and exploitation of intellectual property brings in-house and outside counsel together with strategic decision makers. Executives approach intellectual property (IP) as a tool for converting knowledge into value. They turn to counsel for help in defining and protecting this vital asset.

Intellectual Property: The Basics

Let's start by understanding the distinction between intellectual *capital* and intellectual *property*. The difference is more than semantic: it relates to ownership and legal protections. Intellectual capital refers to the accumulated and accessible knowledge and know-how that resides in a firm. That capital is embedded in the corporation's employees and is therefore portable. An employee who learns how to manage well in different countries or gains a deep understanding of an industry simply takes that capital with him/her upon leaving. Intellectual property refers to the components of intellectual capital that can be defined and protected by law. Unlike intellectual capital, IP belongs to the corporation, not to the individual employee.

IP falls into one of four categories:

1. Patents
2. Copyrights
3. Trademarks/trade dress
4. Trade secrets

Let's look briefly at each category to understand the fundamentals of IP, starting with patents, which are the most tangible type of IP and for most non-media firms have the greatest impact on performance and valuation.

Patents

Of all the IP categories, patents offer the strongest legal protection. Robust patent protection is a key factor in allowing companies to generate profit from innovations. Failure to protect the IP that lies at the core of a new product will allow imitators a free ride, collecting profit on the product without having to invest in research and development.

Good to Know

Most new products are made up of multiple patents and may include trade dress protections as well. Take smartphones. One estimate is that a smartphone may be composed of as many as 250,000 separate pieces of IP. It is no wonder, then, that the smartphone has become "a litigation magnet."

Patents fall into one of three categories:

1. Utility patents cover new, useful, and non-obvious inventions. Utility patents protect "processes," which are essentially methods of making something, and "products," which include machines and material composition—essentially, human-made items. The courts have allowed utility patents to cover a method of doing business, mostly involving software applications.

2. Design patents cover new, original, and ornamental designs. The first-ever design patent, awarded in 1842, was for a new type font invented by George Bruce.

3. Plant patents cover new, distinct, asexually reproducing plants; for example, a thorn-free, long-bearing blackberry plant designed to make harvesting easier.

Patents are published 18 months after filing with the U.S. Patent and Trademark Office (USPTO) and run for 20 years from filing. The publication of a patent reveals the precise mechanisms of the product, process, method, or design being protected.

Copyrights

Copyrights cover works of original authorship, including writing, music, motion pictures, and images. The criteria for qualification as IP are that the work is original, has an author/creator, and is expressed in a tangible medium. Copyright IP has obvious importance to media companies, although many other types of businesses own copyrights on material such as training manuals, T-shirt messages, product labels, computer programs, and website content.

A copyright is a form of IP that typically belongs to its creator. However, if the creator is working under contract, the contractor will likely own the property. The copyright owner has the exclusive right to distribute the work as well as to adapt, display, and perform it—a right that lasts the lifetime of the creator plus 70 years (or a fixed span of 95 years for work made for hire).

The author/creator owns the copyright immediately upon creation of qualifying content, although the next step is often to register the copyright with the U.S. Copyright Office. The author may assign rights to another party. He/she can also make the content available to the public for free.

The creator still retains the copyright, but the content is freely available to anyone.

Just because content is published, it is not necessarily copyrightable. The instruction booklet for assembling a gas grill, for instance, is functional rather than original and therefore not subject to copyright. The same would apply to operating manuals and game instructions. A cookbook is a complex mix of copyrightable and non-copyrightable material. Memories the author has of his grandmother making a dish for him 50 years ago, the cover design, the title, and "substantial literary expression" that describes or explains the recipe are all eligible for copyrighting. But the basics of the recipes themselves—the list of ingredients and the mechanical instructions for preparing them ("add," "stir," "cook until translucent")—will not be copyrightable. Certain foods have been patented—microwavable sponge cake and a technique for making extra smooth mayonnaise, for instance— but these must meet the new, useful, and non-obvious criteria of patents.

Trademarks/Trade Dress

Trademarks are symbols used to differentiate one product from another. A single distinguishing word—Apple, Westlaw—can be protected. So can symbols and other devices, including brand names, logos, product design, and packaging. That would include McDonald's Golden Arches logo, perhaps the best known trademark on the planet, as well as Tiffany's robin's egg blue gift boxes, NBC's three chimes, and the Nike swoosh. The goal in all cases is to allow a corporation to build and capture value from goodwill, and to ensure that customers are able to make an informed purchase without confusion. Thus, a green grocer is free to sell apples despite Apple's trademark because there is no reasonable prospect of customer confusion. Unlike patents, trademark protection is forever, as long as the owner keeps it in active use.

Trade dress is a category of trademarks that covers a broader understanding of nonfunctional but distinguishable design. As with all trademarks, trade

Point of Order

When the Supreme Court addressed trade dress for a fast-food restaurant, it spoke it terms of the "total image" of the business, which included "the shape and general appearance of the exterior of a restaurant, the identifying sign, the interior kitchen floor plan, the decor, the menu, the equipment used to serve food, the servers' uniforms and other features reflecting on the total image of the restaurant."

dress must have an aspect of distinctiveness that customers can identify and in which the owner can build goodwill. UPS's ubiquitous use of brown is an example of trade dress.

Trade dress protection is especially useful for franchise operations: McDonald's, Dunkin' Donuts, and so forth. For a franchise business, in which ownership of and investment in the business are shared by the corporation and the franchisee, it is important to accomplish two goals simultaneously: differentiate one chain from another and ensure that all franchise outlets in the same chain look like they belong together. For that reason, much of what distinguishes one from another—a McDonald's from a Wendy's or a Dunkin' Donuts from a Honey Dew—falls under trade dress.

> ## Point of Order
>
> The trademark implications of Internet domain names have attracted judicial attention in recent years. In 2000, for example, Web-Pro approached Harvard University with a proposition. Web-Pro had registered 68 domain names containing the words "Harvard" or "Radcliffe." Examples included "harvard-doctor.com," "harvard-lawyer.com," and "harvardmba2000.com." Would Harvard be interested in purchasing these registered domain names? Not only did the university decline the offer, it sued for trademark infringement and the court forced Web-Pro to cancel its registration of all domain names carrying the "Harvard" and "Radcliffe" trademarks.

Trade Secrets

Trade secrets—confidential and useful information that has been developed with an investment of time and money and protected by the owner—are a special form of IP. Because there is no federal trade secret law, protection falls to states. To add some uniformity, 46 states have adopted the Uniform Trade Secrets Act. Unlike patents, trade secrets do not have to meet the newness criterion. A corporation may declare any useful information to be a trade secret without proving newness. However, to warrant protection, that secret must be shown to generate economic advantage by virtue of remaining a secret. Additionally, the corporation will need to demonstrate that it has made a reasonable effort to keep the secret a secret. Nondisclosure agreements, limited access, and security measures are all ways to demonstrate a corporation's efforts to ensure secrecy.

Because there is no registration process for trade secrets, legal protection is either preventative (to block the threat of revelation) or remedial (to assess damage after a trade secret has been revealed). Once a corporation

Although trade secrets are not explicitly protected by federal law, there are federal statutes covering many of the activities that would be involved in stealing trade secrets: corporate espionage, computer hacking, conspiracy to steal, and so on.

seeks either prevention or remediation, it must show that the information was not "readily ascertainable": that is, it was not easily visible and discoverable to observers.

It is possible in this age of computer-aided design that anything can be "reversed engineered" and the secret information residing at the core of a trade secret will eventually be revealed. Just what *is* the recipe for KFC's original fried chicken? What *is* it that makes WD-40 work on virtually every known surface? However, the expenditure of vast resources of time, money, and expertise to unearth trade secrets would likely be viewed by the courts as an affirmation of the trade secret's value and justification for keeping it secret.

Point of Order

Different IP protections:
- Patents—20 years from filing
- Copyrights—life of the author plus 70 years
- Trademarks/trade dress—forever, as long as kept in use
- Trade secrets—forever

Trade Secrets versus Patents

Perhaps the most famous and longest-lived trade secret belongs to Coca-Cola: the "Merchandise 7X" formula for Coke. The Coke secret and its longevity help illustrate an important aspect of a trade secret that distinguishes it from a patent. Patents, as already noted, offer the strongest legal protection. They also provide the owner with opportunities to create revenue by selling or leasing them. However, a trade secret has three key advantages over a patent:

1. A trade secret does not have to meet the newness criterion; it just needs to be a valuable secret. It is possible, therefore, that a trade secret would not be patentable.

2. A trade secret does not have to be revealed to gain protection. Patent applications must show explicitly what it is that is being patented—information that will be made public 18 months after filing.

3. A trade secret never expires.

For these reasons, a corporation may, in some instances, prefer to use trade secrets rather than patents.

Patent Trolls

One concern that keeps executives and counsel up at night is the threat of the so-called patent troll. The derogatory term refers to a corporation that amasses a portfolio of patents—often by buying defunct companies specifically for their IP—with the intent to sue or threaten to sue other firms for patent infringement. The goal of the troll is to seek a settlement from a corporation that wishes to avoid the drawn-out, expensive, and uncertain dynamics of a trial. That's why these companies are also called "patent extortionists."

Virginia-based NTP, a patent holding company founded in 1992, is often cited as a model of the patent troll. After NTP failed to license its wireless email patents to several companies, it brought suit against Research In Motion (RIM)—the maker of the BlackBerry—for patent infringement. RIM claimed that it had used public domain technology—that is, technology that was not new but based on publicly available details—but a jury sided with NTP. In addition to awarding damages, the court ordered RIM to cease and desist infringement, a move that would have shut down Black-Berry systems. RIM appealed and the ordered remedies were stayed. Ultimately the USPTO agreed with RIM that the contents of the technology had been published and were therefore not patentable.

The Value of IP

Most businesses generate more than one type of IP. Take McDonald's. Most of us recognize the power and value of the Golden Arches trademark, but as shown in Exhibit 8-1, the company makes claims in all four categories of IP.

Exhibit 8-1: McDonald's IP

IP Category	Example
Patents	Conveyer belt assembly; automated grill; food safety system; dual-compartment sandwich package
Trademarks/ Trade Dress	Golden Arches, Big Mac, Super-Size, Mac Attack, "I'm lovin' it" slogan, Chicken McNuggets, french fry box design, Ronald McDonald, McDonald's building design
Copyrights	Jingles, training manual
Trade Secret	Big Mac "secret sauce"

Like any other property owned by a corporation, IP has value that appears on the balance sheet; in this case, as an intangible asset. The fact that IP is an intangible asset does not detract from the real value it has for its owner. In 2006, when Ford Motor desperately needed to raise capital, it pledged its blue oval trademark as collateral along with tangible assets.[1] So, how does a corporation place value on IP?

The valuation process starts with an audit to determine just what IP is owned and then places a value on that property. In order to do that, accountants will separate core from noncore IP. Core IP protects the corporation's current and future product/service lines. Noncore IP is not being used in current or planned future products. Core IP is then assigned a value as a percentage of the corporation's total market value. That percentage varies depending on the industry. Pharmaceuticals and high technology businesses, for example, will assign a higher percentage of total value to IP than will manufacturers. Still, the percentage will be significant for all businesses.

Complex formulas are available for making these calculations, of course. The point is that IP can account for a significant portion of a firm's total value: often 70 percent or more. In addition to monetary value, IP also provides a business with strategic avenues to generate revenue and seek competitive advantage. So let's turn next to the strategic use of IP.

Strategic Options for IP

Identifying, protecting, and valuing a firm's IP is a preliminary step. Each business faces a number of strategic choices relating to that IP. Those choices can be placed in two broad categories: how to get IP and how to use it.

How to Get IP

Corporations can amass a robust body of IP in many ways. Widely considered to be the world's "patent king," IBM generated over 6,000 patents in 2010 alone. With 8,000 inventors operating in 36 countries, IBM demonstrated the power of internally generated patents. It is important to remember, however, that patent generation by employees is only one method of gaining IP. A "make" strategy—internally generated patents—can be supplemented or substituted by two additional approaches: buy and license.

---

1. Ford never lost the right to use that blue oval trademark.

Make. Firms make their own IP by investing in R&D. Corporations often have R&D units that work in collaboration with divisions to develop new patentable products and processes aimed at meeting specific customer needs. Multinational corporations may operate R&D centers in several countries to take advantage of local and regional brain power. Businesses will also engage in what is known as "pure" research—generic research that does not target an immediate customer need—although this is smaller portion of the total R&D budget. It is not unusual for firms to partner with universities and government-sponsored labs that are more likely to be engaged in pure research.

R&D budgets are typically measured as a percentage of the corporation's total revenues and can range from a low of 0.1 percent for Acer to 14 percent for Microsoft and higher. When looking at these figures, it is important to remember that spending alone does not generate innovation. Just look at the high technology industry. Apple has one of the lowest R&D spending-to-revenue percentages—less than 3 percent—in the industry. Yet when it comes to innovation, Apple outshines many of its competitors. Spending on R&D is important, but the ability to develop new products that will find a market is also based on the corporation's closeness to customers and its capacity for internal collaboration.

Given the high cost of research as well as the uncertainty of a payoff for the efforts (the risk of R&D discussed in Chapter 7), businesses may cooperate with other businesses: sometimes supply chain partners, sometimes even competitors. To speed up development of hybrids, for example, Toyota Motors joined with supply-chain partner Matsushita Electric to create a joint development agreement with the goal of inventing new electronic systems. After forming a joint venture, Panasonic EV Energy, the companies developed 100 patents for hybrids.[2] Competitors, too, occasionally find cooperation advantageous. At the beginning of the satellite radio industry, rivals Sirius and XM entered into a joint development agreement to establish a unified standard for the industry. Both believed that a single standard would be mutually beneficial. The two companies merged in 2008.

---

2. In 2010, the name was changed to Primearth EV Energy to reflect Toyota's growing ownership of the venture.

Point of Order

As in all cases where competitors cooperate, there needs to be sensitivity to antitrust implications.

Point of Order

Key federal antimonopoly statutes:
- Sherman Antitrust Act (1890)— prohibits anti-competitive agreements and actions.
- Clayton Antitrust Act (1914)— prohibits price-fixing, agreements to control supplies, and abuse of corporate power to gain a monopoly.

Many states have adopted statutes to parallel the Sherman Act.

Buy. IP is property and like other forms of property can be bought and sold. Buying and selling patents has become a lively market over the past decade—a way for purchasers to establish a stronger position in their current market or move quickly into a new market, and for sellers to raise revenue. After Borders declared bankruptcy, Barnes & Noble paid nearly $14 million for the defunct corporation's IP, including trademarks, in order to build market strength in its competitive battle with Amazon. Google purchased Motorola Mobility for $12.5 billion, with Motorola's 17,000 patents accounting for at least half that value.

For Google, that purchase supported the corporation's increasing emphasis on mobile technology, while building resources to compete with Apple.

Buyer beware is always an important lesson to remember in these transactions. In 1998, Volkswagen (VW) spent $713 million buying Rolls-Royce Motor Cars from Vickers PLC (the purchase also included Bentley). The VW CEO admitted that much of the incentive for that purchase was to gain ownership of a single piece of IP: the Rolls-Royce double-R trademark that distinguished its cars. But as it turned out, Rolls-Royce Motor Cars (and, as a result, Vickers) did not own the coveted trademark. It was, in fact, the property of a separate Rolls-Royce aerospace company, which had licensed it to Vickers. In what the *New York Times* called "an embarrassing and costly misjudgment," VW watched the trademark go to archrival BMW. In

addition to pointing to the need for due
diligence, the story highlights a third
approach to amassing IP: licensing.

License. Licensing allows one corporation to commercialize the IP (excluding trade secrets) of a second company, typically in return for a royalty. Take Starbucks. Unlike Dunkin' Donuts and McDonald's, Starbucks does not engage in franchising. However, it does license use of its trademarks and patented technology. At Northeastern University, for example, Chartwells manages all of the food-providing services, including a licensed Starbucks operation. The licensing gives Chartwells access to valuable IP it does not own. Starbucks benefits as well, gaining access to locations—it follows the licensing path at many universities, hospitals, and airports—that would otherwise be unavailable.

Corporations occasionally engage in cross-licensing agreements in which participating parties license patents to each other. Cross-licensing can turn two companies into partners, even when they are competitors. IBM and Dell entered a cross-licensing agreement in which IBM licensed some processes from Dell and offered IBM components to Dell at lower-than-market prices. P&G and Glad created a collaborative agreement when P&G combined its Press'n Seal technology with Glad's market leading Glad Wrap to create "Glad Press'n Seal."

How to Use IP

However it is amassed, IP is considered to be a strategic asset for a business. The next question is how to deploy that asset. The options for exploiting IP fall into one of three categories: keep/protect/exploit, license and sell, and give away.

Keep/protect/exploit. Bringing a patent to market in the form of a new product or an improvement on an existing product is the most obvious route to commercialization. To be proactive, companies can scan for existing patents before bringing a product to market, sometimes even before making investments in new product development. Even though an invention must meet the newness criterion to receive a patent, the product will most likely be entering an arena with other related patents.

Before embarking on a new product development process, executives and their legal counsel can ask a number of questions:

- Is our new product likely to give us competitive advantage?

- Is our new product likely to be challenged legally for patent infringement?

- Do we have an ample opportunity for patent-protected product improvement?

Businesses may decide to build what is known as a patent fence around a new product by making sure they—and not their competitors—own related patents that might come into play as substitute products in the future.

Point of Order

Before embarking on new product development, executives and IP lawyers survey the state of patents— What are they? Who owns them?— that relate to the product.

The ability to establish market position through patents is often a key element in making strategic decisions for companies. Gillette works with product development people and patent attorneys to choose among multiple blade designs only after a full patent analysis. It then builds a patent fence of multiple interlocking patents to make duplication by competitors difficult.

License and Sell. Corporations also use IP as a source of revenue by mining their existing stockpile of IP (again, excluding trade secrets) for licensing or sale. Xerox created a separate business unit for that purpose. "If you only use your patents to protect your products, which is the old paradigm, you're missing all manner of revenue-generating and other opportunities," said Xerox's CEO.[3] As we saw earlier, Starbucks licenses IP to increase its

---

3. Quoted in Kevin G. Rivette and D. Kevin, "Discovering New Value in Intellectual Property." *Harvard Business Review* (January–February 2000), p. 7.

point-of-sale opportunities. Even nonprofits can generate revenue through licensing. Sesame Workshop (formerly the Children's Television Workshop) has been successful in licensing its Sesame Street trademarks—most especially Elmo—to for-profit companies. Licensing may also be a strategic choice if the company hopes to create a de facto industry standard. Qualcomm, a wireless and modular technology company, licensed its code division multiple access (CDMA) to create a new industry standard and make its own patented products more appealing.

Even when a firm decides to license, it still faces choices. Take two biotechnology firms. CAT restricted its licensing of its antibody technology to a few large pharmaceutical companies such as Eli Lilly and Pfizer, which allowed CAT to collect large royalties while minimizing the costs associated with monitoring activities. Dynax took a different approach to its antibody display libraries, licensing to many and diverse companies while carefully avoiding direct competitors.

The selling of patents provides another opportunity to raise capital. In 2011 the defunct Nortel Networks of Canada raised $4.5 billion by selling over 6,000 patents to technology companies, including Apple, Microsoft, and RIM. AOL was able to sell over 800 patents to Microsoft and use that capital to build its own media holdings, including the acquisition of the *Huffington Post*. Those patents involved search, email, and instant messaging, many of which came into AOL's possession when it bought Netscape in 1998.

Give Away. Giving away IP may seem counterintuitive. After a corporation has invested in amassing and protecting IP, why give it away? In fact, a number of businesses do just that for certain portions of their IP. Giving away IP eliminates protection costs. IBM has, over the past several years, increased the number of inventions it publishes through technical papers and on the Internet rather than patenting. This so-called defensive publishing gives away internally developed IP while protecting against any other corporation patenting the same invention.

Choosing to make IP "public domain" is also a strategy used to stimulate the development of complementary assets by others. Apple, Google, Amazon, and Facebook give away strategically selected IP with the goal of encouraging developers to build compatible applications that will make their own patented systems more competitive. In 2005 IBM made 500 patents available to the open-source software community in hopes of stimulating innovations that would be mutually valuable.

Finally—Why IP Matters

Because we live—and businesses compete—in a knowledge-based economy, IP has become an indispensable asset. Top-level executives, even board members, are increasingly involved in IP management: making decisions about attractiveness of market spaces based in part on the IP landscape, defending and enhancing corporate reputation in terms of potential IP litigation, and setting rules and procedures for managing IP within units to ensure projects take full accounting of salient legal issues. IP has great potential to increase a business's innovativeness and generate revenues. The potential is also there for litigious battles with challengers. For all these reasons, the effective management of IP needs to be embedded in a thorough understanding of the laws and an appreciation of the opportunities.

Back of the Envelope Notes

Four types of IP:
1. Patents
2. Copyrights
3. Trademarks/trade dress
4. Trade secrets

••••••••••••••••••••••

Trade dress is especially useful for franchise operations.

••••••••••••••••••••••

IP is valued as part of a corporation's total assets.

••••••••••••••••••••••

Corporation can amass IP in one or more of three ways:
1. Make
2. Buy
3. License

••••••••••••••••••••••

R&D budget is typically stated as a percentage of total revenues. But remember, innovation is about more than the size of an R&D budget.

••••••••••••••••••••••••

Competitors can occasionally share IP.

••••••••••••••••••••••••

Companies can raise capital by licensing and selling patents.

••••••••••••••••••••••••

There are times when "giving away" IP makes good strategic sense.

CHAPTER **9**

MERGERS, ACQUISITIONS, AND IPOS

Mergers and acquisitions (M&As) and initial public offerings (IPOs) are among the most significant, complex, and legally dense transactions in which corporations engage. At every step of the process, counsel plays a vital role: conducting due diligence, structuring deals, representing the corporate client in negotiations among the numerous parties, and ensuring compliance with prevailing laws and regulations. M&A transactions quite often lead to follow-up litigation, including shareholder suits. Individual lawyers and firms can make their reputations on M&A and IPO expertise. Even in times when the pace of such large transactions slows, billings provide an important source of revenue for firms.

Prior to becoming immersed in the complexity of these transactions, it is useful to take a step back. M&A and IPOs are critical elements of corporate strategy. Decisions to acquire a new business or to transform from a private to a public corporation will have a significant impact on the future competitiveness of the company.

The Role of Mergers and Acquisitions

Executives use the terms "merger" and "acquisition" interchangeably, typically as a single phrase: M&A. For most of the chapter, I will follow that managerial practice. It is, however, important to recognize that, as defined by state law and regulated by the SEC, there are distinctions between mergers and acquisitions. Counsel will be needed to help construct the transaction to meet the needs and obligations of the involved parties.

The SEC defines a merger as a transaction that combines two or more corporations into a single entity. Most states require that a merger be approved by at least a majority of the shareholders of the involved corporations. The result of a merger between corporations is that the surviving entity assumes all of the liabilities and obligations of the entity (or entities) that cease to exist.

Corporate executives may wish to avoid the shareholder vote required of a merger. Shareholder votes typically take months to organize and run. In addition, there may be a risk of a shareholder battle over a particular transaction. In that case, the corporation may instead pursue an acquisition, which does *not* require approval of either company's shareholders. The acquiring company, known as the "bidder," may purchase assets— real estate, machinery, inventory, intellectual property, and so on—of the acquired company, known as the "target," without purchasing any of the target's stock. An acquisition may also involve the purchase of the target's stock without the assumption of the target's liabilities. The statutes, court rulings, and SEC regulations that establish the requirements of shareholder approval are complex and can vary from state to state. Although the distinctions between how a merger or an acquisition can proceed are significant, the end result remains largely the same. The target ceases to exist as an independent entity and the bidder now controls the expanded corporation.

Bidders will be attracted to potential targets when they are undervalued. Assigning a valuation to a potential acquisition is a complex matter. One common approach involves

> ## Point of Order
>
> In a merger, only one corporation is designated to be the surviving entity. That surviving entity assumes all property, contract rights, and liabilities of the non-surviving firm. The name of the resulting entity may be substituted in any legal proceeding undertaken by the non-surviving entity. In an acquisition, the bidder and target will negotiate the disposition of liabilities.

replacement value. What would be the cost of replacing all the assets of the potential target from scratch? Bidders often rely on a calculation known as the q-ratio, which is the ratio of the market value of a firm to the replacement costs of its assets. When the q-ratio is less than 1, the market value of the target as a whole is below the cost of buying its parts. Firms with a q-ratio below 1 offer an inviting target. With a ratio above 1, potential bidders would often prefer to buy specific assets—say, a factory or a patent—than the whole firm.

> ### Good to Know
>
> The numbers needed to calculate a firm's q-ratio are provided by the Federal Reserve and updated quarterly (FRB Z.1. Flow of Funds Accounts of the United States).

M&A Strategy

When corporations look for companies to acquire, they follow one of five M&A strategies:

- A *horizontal* M&A brings together two former competitors. When Starbucks first entered the New England region, for example, it faced intense competition from a local chain, Coffee Connection. Eventually, Starbucks bought Coffee Connection and rebranded all of its stores as Starbucks.

- A *vertical* M&A involves one corporation buying another that had been part of its supply chain. For example, in 2010 Apple acquired Siri, Inc., a company started three years earlier that had developed software that incorporated voice recognition to act as an intelligent personal assistant. Apple then integrated Siri into its next-generation iPhone.

- A *resource-based* M&A in which one corporation purchases another to gain access to valuable resources. When Kellogg purchased Keebler snack foods, for example, the acquisition was motivated largely by a desire to take possession of a key Keebler resource. The snack food company had a delivery system that brought its products directly to retailers, while Kellogg operated through a less efficient warehouse system.

- A *market extension* M&A allows the acquiring corporation to extend its own market by moving up- or down-market, as when Gap acquired Banana Republic to extend its market into a luxury brand. A market extension can also occur when one corporation acquires another in a new country or geographic location, as when Starbucks acquired Seattle Coffee's U.K.-based subsidiary.

- A *conglomerate* M&A involves a corporation acquiring another with which it has no previous relationship but that simply offers a good investment opportunity, such as when Berkshire Hathaway purchased Jordan Furniture or Philip Morris purchased Kraft. In these cases, the corporations are following the unrelated diversification strategy discussed in Chapter 3.

The strategies (summarized in Exhibit 9-1) may overlap. For example, when Kellogg acquired Keebler for its resources, it was also engaging in market extension by moving into the salty snack market.

Exhibit 9-1: Five M&A Strategies

Type	Definition	Example
Horizontal M&A	Combines two former competitors	Sirius and XM Satellite Radio merge
Vertical M&A	Combines two supply chain partners	Apple acquires Siri, Inc.
Resource-based M&A	Purchases significant resources possessed by the target	Kellogg acquires Keebler
Market extension M&A	Purchases a company with a different market position in the same industry or a different geographic base	Gap acquires Banana Republic (different market position); Starbucks acquires Seattle Coffee's U.K. subsidiary (different geographic base)
Conglomerate M&A	Acquires unrelated business as an investment	Berkshire Hathaway acquires Jordan Furniture

The most common rationale for an M&A is the benefit of synergy. When functions can be shared—mostly back-office functions like credit and billing, information technology, and logistics—firms can gain advantage from the economies of scale. When the same activity is conducted over and over, the marginal cost of doing it one more time is far less than it was at the beginning. Take the TJX purchase of Marshalls. At the time, TJX operated T.J. Maxx as a discount clothing operation. By purchasing a competitor—a horizontal M&A—TJX could streamline some of the services associated with operating a retail business. There would be one credit office for both T.J. Maxx and Marshalls, for example. Based on the economies of scale, the unified function would operate less expensively than two separate offices performing the same activities. TJX expanded the economies of scale advantage even further as it opened more discount retailing businesses.

The M&A Transaction

Once the strategic process of selecting a target is completed, corporations face the choice of how to finance the purchase. The purchase of the target can be done with cash, stock, or some combination of the two. A cash deal is exactly what it sounds like; cash is paid to purchase the target's stock and thus take possession of its assets. In a true acquisition, cash will be paid for the target's assets but not necessarily its stock. It is the cleanest and quickest option and one of the primary reasons companies like to keep cash on hand. The bidder may want to retain some executives and key employees and can encourage them to stay by offering a retention bonus. However, all the governance power remains with the bidder.

In a stock deal, the purchase occurs in the form of trading bidder stock for target stock. Thus, all shareholders in the target corporation are given an equity position in the bidder corporation. There are a number of advantages to a stock deal. For one, the bidder does not have to raise and spend cash, thus avoiding debt or depleting its cash reserves. Stock deals also have tax advantages over cash deals.

On the other hand, a stock deal inevitably dilutes the control that the bidder's shareholders had before the transaction. Put simply, the original shareholders now own a smaller proportion of the corporation—and will receive proportionately less of a return in the form of dividends—than they did previously. Of course, if the M&A transaction works out advantageously, all shareholders will benefit.

However the deal is structured, the bidder must do due diligence to determine the value of the target. A team composed of lawyers, accountants, financial specialists, human resource experts, and management personnel will investigate all aspects the target's operations and finances. Due diligence focuses on a financial review of assets and liabilities, revenues and expenses, and so on. The bidder will also want to assess the quality of the target's top management team, the state of its technology, and the capabilities embedded in its employees.

One of the most important due diligence tasks is to confirm that the target has clear and uncontested ownership of key assets, including intellectual property. Remember the cautionary tale from Chapter 8 about VW thinking it had purchased the Rolls-Royce double-R logo and then watching it go instead to rival automaker BMW? These are matters that must be handled in the due diligence phase of the transaction, and a primary reason for including counsel on the due diligence team.

Typically, when the bidder is purchasing all of the target's stock, it will pay an acquisition premium; that is, it will pay over market value for the stock. In 2008, for example, Mars bought Wrigley in order to compete with the increasingly powerful Cadbury Schweppes. This was a cash deal in which Mars paid a 28 percent acquisition premium (i.e., 28 percent above Wrigley's stock price at the time of the deal). Those premiums are designed to make the deal collaborative and quick. The downside risk— remember, every important decision carries risk—arises from the fact that the premium may not be fully earned back once the two companies are combined.

Friendly versus Hostile Transaction. In a friendly M&A, the bidder is invited to bid by the target's CEO and board. A hostile takeover occurs when the target's board is not soliciting a bid. Hostile takeovers may have their roots in more friendly negotiations. Microsoft's ultimately unsuccessful 2008 hostile bid to acquire Yahoo!, for example, came about after friendly talks fell apart.

The hostile bidder may begin the takeover process by purchasing large blocks of the target's stock. Because a hostile bid is opposed by the target's board, the act of acquiring stock will help the bidder pressure the board to sell. The bidder will often accompany its uninvited offer with a public letter intended to induce the target's shareholders to support the bid. This public letter, referred to as a bear hug, suggests that the offer may be too good for the shareholders to pass up.

Boards often take preventative steps to make their companies less susceptible to an unwelcome takeover. Common defenses against takeovers can be placed in one of three categories:

- *Poison pills*—a provision automatically triggered when the holdings of a hostile party reach a predetermined level, say 15 percent to 20 percent, of total outstanding stock. A poison pill provision gives existing shareholders the right to purchase additional shares at reduced prices with the goal of diluting the power of the hostile party.

- *Shark repellents*—a variety of defenses written into a corporation's bylaws that make it difficult for a hostile party to gain control of the board. These include staggering board elections so that only a minority of directors is up for re-election at any one time and limiting shareholder actions that can be undertaken without board approval.

- *Greenmail*—an offer by the target to the hostile bidder to pay the bidder to withdraw its offer and refrain from any further actions. This may include buying back stock that the hostile bidder has already acquired at an above-market price.

When all else fails, boards may turn to a white knight—that is, a corporation or private equity firm that is invited by the target board to step in and engage in a friendly rather than hostile takeover.

In using devices such as these to fend off unwelcome advances, boards cannot lose focus on their responsibility to shareholders. Microsoft's hostile bid for Yahoo! represented a 62 percent acquisition premium over Yahoo!'s market value at the time. Yahoo! executives maintained the corporation was worth more.[1] But was it really in Yahoo! shareholders' best interest to say no? A year later, Yahoo!'s stock stood at just under $9 a share; Microsoft had reportedly offered $33. When shareholders feel that the board and

---

1. Microsoft could have made a tender offer directly to shareholders in hopes of fermenting a shareholder fight. Instead it withdrew its offer.

CEO are motivated mainly to hold onto their control rather than to benefit shareholders, they may mount lawsuits and/or challenges to incumbent board members.

Going Public

Firms also face a key strategic question concerning whether to be private or "go public" through an initial public offering. Like M&A transactions, the IPO process is complex, costly, and demanding, requiring a great deal of expertise, including legal and financial support. The IPO process applies most frequently to entrepreneurial startups that—assuming they are successful—will eventually face the private/public choice. To understand the dynamics of that choice, it is vital to appreciate the distinction between a public and a private corporation.

A public corporation is one that trades its stock publicly through an existing exchange or an over-the-counter network. Private companies do not offer stock to the public. By avoiding the public sale of stock, private companies are exempt from the myriad laws imposed on public companies—SOX

Point of Order

Beyond the due diligence phase, a complex web of legal and regulatory frameworks surrounds any M&A transaction. Federal securities laws and state anti-takeover laws must be taken into account. Especially in a horizontal transaction where two former competitors combine, particular care will need to be taken to ensure compliance with federal and state antitrust laws. In addition, some industries—banking, communications, defense, and public utilities among them—are the focus of particular laws that must also be followed. Stock-based purchases are also likely to raise tricky governance issues in the post-transaction period that lawyers can anticipate and plan for. Finally, lawsuits filed on behalf of minority shareholders often follow a transaction.

Point of Order

State anti-takeover statutes are designed to protect firms from hostile bidders, typically by limiting the bidder's ability to go around the target's board and put pressure directly on the shareholders.

and Dodd-Frank among them—as well as the rules and regulations imposed by the SEC and various stock exchanges.

IPO Strategy

Although exempt from laws regulating public companies, private companies do have regulations to abide by. The one that most directly impacts the IPO decision is the U.S. Securities Exchange Act of 1934, which requires that, once a corporation reaches 500 shareholders, it must file with the SEC. It does not have to hold an IPO and become a publicly traded company. However, it must comply with all SEC requirements. No matter how big a firm becomes in terms of revenue and employees, as long as it structures its ownership so that it has fewer than 500 shareholders, it can avoid the requirements of public reporting.

By far, the most attractive aspect of being a public company is access to capital through stock markets. There are other benefits as well. Many executives believe that being a publicly traded company, especially one listed on a major exchange, will build prestige that can be valuable in attracting both suppliers and customers. Founders may also wish to enlarge their base of shareholders by granting employees an ownership position in the company. Stock ownership by employees is considered a reward for past efforts and a motivator of future performance.

Good to Know

It is fair to assume that most large corporations are public; most, but not all. *Forbes* lists Cargill—a multinational agribusiness with over $100 billion in annual sales—as the largest private company in the United States. Cargill has remained private by tightly controlling its ownership to a small number of descendants of the founder. Other notable private companies include Mars, Bechtel, Enterprise Rent-A-Car, Wegmans, and In-N-Out Burger.

Good to Know

Companies may also go from public to private. The management may buy back all the outstanding stock by borrowing money, a leveraged buyout (LBO). A private equity firm may buy the company with the plan to increase the firm's value and then take it public again through an IPO.

Still, there are a number of issues that need to be considered prior to embarking on an IPO. The process itself is costly and time consuming. One estimate suggests that 10 percent of the total amount raised through an IPO will go to law firms, accountants, and bankers in fees. Another estimate suggests that the CEO will be required to devote as much as 30 hours a week for six months to the process—a major commitment that will involve other executives as well. Then, too, the existing shareholders, often founders and family members, will lose their complete control over the business once it becomes public. In addition, public firms are subject to the kind of scrutiny—not to mention regulation and compliance requirements—that privates can avoid. Public stock is vulnerable to manipulation by short-sellers who hope to profit from a declining stock price. And finally, the IPO process requires public disclosure of the company's financial accounts, a disclosure that some private owners prefer to avoid.

Once those advantages and disadvantages are weighed (see Exhibit 9-2 for a summary), the decision to go forward with an IPO follows some standard guidelines.

Exhibit 9-2: Advantages and Disadvantages of "Going Public"

Advantages	Disadvantages
Access to capital	A costly, time-consuming process
A payoff for founders	Dilution of control
Sharing ownership with employees	Public scrutiny and regulation that applies to public companies, and the opportunity for stock manipulation
Prestige	Requirement to disclose financials

The IPO Transaction

A decision to undertake an IPO will lead immediately to a required filing with the SEC: Form S-1. That filing amounts to a prospectus—similar to a 10-K report—that details the firm's financial and operational status. Once it is filed, that prospectus becomes public and is used in presenting the corporation to potential investors.

Point of Order

The SEC's approval of a corporation's S-1 request to undertake an IPO does not denote any assessment of the price being placed on the initial offering, just that the company is in compliance with all necessary procedures.

Once the S-1 filing has been made, the SEC imposes a "quiet period" that lasts until it officially sanctions the transaction. During that period, company executives and their representatives are barred from advocating for their company or its value. They may, however, disclose financials and other facts intended to help potential bidders assess the value of the company.

Good to Know

Appropriate conduct during the quiet period is not always obvious, as Google discovered prior to its 2004 IPO. Google founders Larry Page and Sergey Brin had granted an interview to *Playboy* that took place before Google's S-1 filing. It appeared in print, however, during the enforced quiet period and could easily have been interpreted as "jumping the gun"—that is, advocating during the quiet period. The SEC could have forced a postponement of the IPO. To prevent this, Google's attorneys worked with SEC regulators to make the entire interview available to all potential bidders.

Making Book. The company will need to select an investment bank to act as the underwriter of the transaction. For any large IPO, there will be multiple banks and brokerage houses that make up the syndicate handling the transaction. One bank will be designated as the lead underwriter and spearhead the effort to sell stock publicly. The underwriter will also conduct due diligence on the company as part of its effort to determine its value. Setting a value shapes how much the underwriter plans to raise in the IPO and at what price to set the initial stock offer.

Ultimately, of course, the initial stock price will need to reflect buyers' willingness to pay. To gain input from the market—mainly from institutional investors such as pension funds, hedge funds, financial advisors, mutual funds, and the like—the underwriter will undertake a book-building process. IPO underwriters organize a road show, with the occasional participation of company executives, that explains the company's valuation and tests interest in the stock. By keeping track of all expressions of interest in the stock, the underwriters can set the opening stock price.

The process of selecting the opening price to place on a share is full of uncertainties. Most typically, the stock is initially undervalued. In that case, the stock price rises dramatically following the opening of sales. Less frequent is overpricing, in which the stock price actually falls during the first days and weeks of sales. In that case, the reputation of the underwriter suffers, and it often spends its own money to prop up the stock price.

Good to Know

Some firms—Google being the most recent prominent example—use an auction in their IPO process rather than the more traditional book-building process.

Good to Know

In perhaps the most dramatic recent example of overpricing, Facebook's 2012 IPO opened at $38 a share. In the weeks and months that followed, the share price plummeted—it stood at $18.06 three months later—and Facebook's market capitalization shed $50 billion. Facebook's lead underwriter, Morgan Stanley, experienced losses in the process, as did many other institutional investors. Even NASDAQ, Facebook's exchange, suffered as glitches in the mechanics of the opening day's trading forced the exchange to cover some of the losses.

Good to Know

A lead underwriter may sign a "firm commitment" agreement with the company in which the underwriter agrees, once the initial price is set, to buy all the stock and then sell it. In this case, it is the underwriter who bears the risk if the stock price should fall and enjoys the benefit if the price climbs.

Corporate Cleanup. A key legal responsibility involves corporate cleanup. Counsel will need to review all minutes from the firm's board as well as shareholder meetings. Counsel will also want to be sure that all intellectual property has been properly accounted for and protected, and all formal agreements and contracts between the company and other parties are in order. In addition, attorneys will help bring all articles of incorporation and governance arrangements up to compliance with the requirements of a public company.

Point of Order

Legal fees are second only to the money paid out to underwriters during the IPO process.

Point of Order

The process of incorporating requires the filing of a charter with the chosen state of incorporation. That charter typically includes articles of incorporation, which are the basic governing rules for the corporation. The charter becomes the principal contract that binds the corporation.

Finally—Why M&As and IPOs Matter

M&A and IPO activities represent complex transactions that require executives to work closely with a wide array of specialists: accountants, financial managers, investment bankers, and lawyers. There are transactions that represent significant costs for the corporation and generate significant fees for outside counsel. Beyond the details—as critical as they are to the success of the transactions—lie strategic decisions impacting the future of the company. M&As and IPOs are, after all, among the most important initiatives a company can undertake.

An M&A is undertaken to expand a company's market, gain access to new products or services, buy capabilities that would be too costly and time consuming to develop on its own, enter new markets, or operate more efficiently—or often, some combination of those reasons. Likewise, the decision to evolve from a private to a public company presents an opportunity to attract capital and a new requirement to comply with public laws and regulations.

Once these decisions are made, the structure of the transactions becomes vital. This is where counsel and others work to ensure that the transaction is structured in a way that maximizes the opportunity for the corporation to reach its goals. By paying attention to the best interests of the corporation during the unfolding of the deal and the manner in which the post-transaction corporation will operate, legal counsel can help shape the desired outcome.

Back of the Envelope Notes

The terms "merger" and "acquisition" are often used interchangeably, but they are different:

- A merger involves the combination of two or more entities into a single corporation and typically requires shareholder approval of both (all) entities.
- An acquisition involves the purchase of either assets or stock of one company by another and may not require shareholder approval.

Specific rules and regulations can vary from state to state.

•••••••••••••••••••••••

M&As can be paid for with cash, stock, or some combination of the two.

•••••••••••••••••••••••

An all-stock transaction eliminates the need to spend huge amounts of cash upfront and has some tax advantages. However, it dilutes the control the original stockholders have over the acquiring company and may be less desirable in the long run.

•••••••••••••••••••••••

A public company is one that trades its stock publicly through an existing exchange or over-the-counter network. Private companies do not offer stock to the public, and so avoid the myriad laws imposed on public companies as well as the rules and regulations imposed by various stock exchanges.

•••••••••••••••••••••••

One of the most important due diligence tasks in an M&A involves ensuring that the target has clear and uncontested ownership of key assets, including IP.

•••••••••••••••••••••••

Typically, the bidder pays an acquisition premium for the target's stock—that is, a price for the stock over what it is then selling for on the market. That premium is intended to speed up the process.

•••••••••••••••••••••••

Once a corporation reaches 500 shareholders, it is legally obligated to file with the SEC and comply with laws covering public companies. It does not, however, have to offer an IPO and sell its stock publicly.

· ·

The formal IPO commences with a required filing with the SEC: Form S-1. That filing amounts to a prospectus that details the firm's financial and operational status. Once it is filed, that prospectus becomes public and is used in presenting the company to potential investors.

· ·

The book-building process involves the lead underwriter gauging institutional interest in the new stock, a process that is used in setting the initial price at which the stock will be offered.

APPENDIX

TALKING THE TALK

Every profession relies on its own specialized vocabulary. For attorneys—both in-house and outside counsel—familiarity with the "talk" of managers should help immeasurably in understanding interactions. Here, therefore, is a list with definitions of key words.

A

Accounting equation—assets = liabilities + shareholders' equity.

Accrual accounting—an approach to accounting followed in the United States that records the economic impact of a transaction when that transaction is agreed to rather than when the cash is received.

Acquisition—a transaction in which one corporation buys assets or shares of another corporation.

Acquisition premium—the difference between the price per share the bidder offers for the target's stock and the pre-acquisition price of that stock.

AIO dimensions—a segmentation of customers based on lifestyle: activities, interests, and opinions.

Asset—a holding of a corporation that can be either converted to cash or put to productive use.

B

Backward integration—a form of vertical integration in which the corporation buys or starts up businesses that serve as suppliers to its other businesses.

Barrier to entry—the level of difficulty faced by a company attempting to enter an industry, including the capital requirement of doing so.

Bear hug—a maneuver in a hostile takeover attempt in which the bidder publishes a letter making an offer intended to entice shareholders who might, in turn, place pressure on the target's board to sell.

Beta (ß)—a measure of a company's stock price volatility relative to the overall market.

Bidder—the designation for a corporation seeking to make an acquisition.

Board book—the briefing book prepared prior to each board meeting.

Board of directors—the mix of independent and non-independent individuals who represent shareholders and oversee the corporation.

Bond—a financial instrument issued by a corporation that is used to borrow money from the purchaser with a predetermined interest rate and payoff schedule.

Bonus—a payment above and beyond salary that is contingent on some measure of performance.

Book-building—the process of gauging interest on the part of potential investors in a stock as part of the IPO process.

Bottom line—a reference to the net income (profit) of a corporation.

Break-even analysis—a determination of the point at which the price of a product will cover the total cost of producing and delivering that product at various sales volumes.

Breakup value—an assessment of how much value each asset of a corporation, including its businesses, would fetch on the open market if sold separately.

Business model—the manner in which a business links activities to deliver a product/service to customers to generate revenue.

B2B (business to business)—a strategy that involves focusing on other businesses as customers.

B2C (business to consumer)—a strategy that involves focusing on end users as customers.

C

Capital market—the system in which individuals and institutions supply capital to corporations by loaning money and/or purchasing equity.

Care duty—the duty of members of the board of directors to stay informed and make deliberate and carefully considered decisions on behalf of the corporation.

Cash cow—a business in the portfolio of a multi-business corporation that can generate revenue without significant new investment.

Cash flow—the amount of cash that moves into or out of a business during a specified period of time.

C-Corporation (often, C-Corp)—the typical form of corporation that enables the corporate entity to be taxed independently of its owners.

Chief executive officer (CEO)—the corporation's top executive who typically sits on the board of directors, sometimes serving as board chairman.

Chief financial officer (CFO)—the corporate executive responsible for overseeing all financial activities in a company.

Clayton Antitrust Act (1914)—prohibits price fixing, agreements to control supplies, and abuse of corporate power to gain a monopoly.

Committee of Sponsoring Organizations of the Treadway Commission (COSO)—a voluntary private-sector organization that created a model used by over 80 percent of public corporations as the standard to assess financial controls.

Commodity—a product class for which features and capabilities are indistinguishable.

Common stock—a class of stock that confers voting rights on the owner.

Compensation—policies related to the design of pay systems.

Compensation and Disclosure Analysis (C&DA)—a disclosure required by the SEC of public corporations concerning executive compensation.

Competitive advantage—the factors that allow one business to be successful in contrast to its rivals.

Consolidated statement—a financial statement that includes data from all the units and divisions in the corporation.

Copyright—a form of intellectual property that protects original works that have an author/creator and are expressed in a tangible medium.

Core IP—intellectual property that protects the corporation's current and future product and service lines.

Corporate brand—an identity or image developed by the corporation that attaches itself to the different businesses in the corporation.

Corporate cleanup—a legal review conducted prior to an IPO designed to ensure that all corporate documents are in order.

Corporate governance—the framework employed by a corporation to guide and control its activities in compliance with prevailing laws and regulations.

Corporation—the legal entity with the responsibility to oversee operations, performance, and accountabilities.

Cost of capital—how much a company must pay in exchange for receiving capital.

Cost-plus pricing—pricing decisions that start with the cost to make a product and add a desired profit margin.

Culture—the pervasive assumptions within an organization concerning how employees ought to behave.

C-Suite—the top executives who manage corporate responsibilities, including the chief executive officer (CEO), chief operating officer (COO), chief financial officer (CFO), chief marketing officer (CMO), chief technology officer (CTO), and general counsel (GC).

Customer division—a corporate unit divided up according to different customer segments.

Customer equity—the net present value of the anticipated lifetime of revenue from a customer minus acquisition and retention costs.

Customer relationship management—systems and processes built for measuring customer habits and behaviors with the goal of increasing customer retention.

D

Derived demand—demand for a company's product that is based on the demand of end purchasers of the product rather than sales channel intermediaries.

Design patent—a patent for a new, original, and ornamental design.

Directors—individuals who serve on a corporation's board and act as the main intermediary between shareholders and corporate officers.

Discounted cash flow—a calculation for determining the value of future cash flows in current dollars.

Diversification—a corporate strategy designed to create value by operating in multiple industries or market segments.

Dividend—a payment made to shareholders from net income declared at the discretion of the board.

Divisional structure—the subdivisions within a multi-business corporation created for the different business units.

Dodd-Frank Wall Street Reform Act (Dodd-Frank)—2010 legislation that imposed enhanced early-warning systems, transparency, and accountability on executives in the financial services sector.

Dotted-line relationship—an indirect reporting relationship between two individuals that requires the subordinate to stay in touch with and be responsive to the superior.

Double-entry bookkeeping—a reference to the requirement that the impact of all transactions be recorded in at least two of three columns in the accounting equation: assets, liabilities, and/or shareholders' equity.

Downside risk—the potential negative impact of uncertainty on outcomes.

Downsize—a corporate action designed to shed assets and/or lay off personnel.

Dual-class stocks—the practice of dividing common stock into different classes and granting one class greater voting power than the other.

E

Economies of scale—the cost advantage derived from a decrease in the cost per unit of an activity as the number of times the activity is performed increases.

Emergency Economic Stabilization Act—2008 legislation that set oversight rules, including restrictions on executive pay, for corporations that accepted government relief as part of the economic recovery.

Employee development—explicit efforts undertaken by a business to help employees develop new skills and competencies.

Employee flow—policies related to the movement of people into, through, and out of the company.

Employee selection—policies related to the process of recruiting and hiring personnel.

Enterprise risk—the combined risk portfolio of the entire corporation.

Exercise price—the price at which an option may be purchased.

Express warranty—a statement of fact and/or promise that a seller makes about a product.

F

Federal Trade Commission Act (1914)—requires that advertising be truthful and fair.

Fiduciary responsibility—the legal responsibility of board members to act on behalf of the best interests of the corporation.

Financial Accounting Standards Board (FASB)—a private organization designated by the SEC to establish GAAP rules governing the preparation of financial reports by non-governmental entities.

Financial controls—the internal systems and procedures designed to ensure that all financial reporting is done properly and accurately.

Five Forces—a frequently used model devised by Michael Porter for analyzing the dynamics of a particular industry.

Foreign direct investment (FDI)—a strategy for entering a foreign market in which the corporation makes a direct capital investment in its overseas expansion.

Forward integration—a form of vertical integration in which the corporation buys or starts up businesses that serve as the distributors and sellers of products produced by its current businesses.

Four P's—a frequently used classification system—referring to product, price, place, and promotion—devised by E. Jerome McCarthy for capturing core marketing activities.

Franchising—a business arrangement in which a corporation sells the rights to its product/services to a franchisee who invests money and agrees to follow rules set by the franchiser.

Friendly bid—a takeover bid invited by and done in collaboration with the target's board and executives.

G

General counsel (GC)—the chief legal officer of the corporation.

Generally accepted accounting principles (GAAP)—a codification of the accounting rules followed by U.S. firms.

Geographic division—a corporate unit divided according to the regions of the world in which it operates.

Green metrics—specific objective measurements of social and environmental impact.

Greenmail—a defense against hostile takeover attempts that involves an offer by the target to pay the bidder to withdraw its bid and refrain from any further actions.

H

Horizontal price fixing—a collaboration among two or more competitors to set prices for a product or service in a way that contravenes market forces.

Hostile bid—a takeover bid that is not invited and that is actively opposed by the target's board and executives.

Human resource management (HRM)—policies regarding the management of people in organizations.

I

Implied warranty—an implicit promise by a merchant that goods are reasonably fit for the purpose for which they are being sold.

Income statement—an accounting of a firm's bottom-line performance.

Independent auditor—an accounting organization certified by the Public Company Accounting Oversight Board that scrutinizes the financial control systems of corporations and issues a report as part of the corporation's 10-K filing that certifies the strength of those controls.

Independent director—a member of the board who is not currently employed or has not recently been employed by the company.

Initial public offering (IPO)—the process by which a formerly private company first offers shares for public purchase.

Inside director—a member of the board who is currently employed at the company.

Intangible product attributes—the non-physical characteristics of a product that elicit a psychological and emotional response from users.

Intellectual capital—the accumulated and accessible knowledge and know-how that resides in a firm.

Intellectual property (IP)—the portion of intellectual capital that can be protected by law.

J

Joint development agreement—an agreement between two or more companies to collaborate in research and development and share any resulting intellectual property.

L

Large-cap corporation—a corporation with a market capitalization of over $10 billion.

Lead director—an independent director selected to oversee independent-only board meetings.

Legal process outsourcing (LPO)—the practice of outsourcing legal services by a law firm, often accompanied by offshoring.

Leveraged buyout (LBO)—a purchase of company stock by managers financed through debt; a typical approach to taking a public company private.

Liability—an obligation the corporation has to make payments.

Limited liability company (LLC)—a business form typically used for small businesses with few if any employees that limits the liability of the owner(s) and does not allow for the issuance of stock.

Liquidity—a measure of the capacity of an asset to be turned into cash quickly and with low transaction costs.

LLC member—the designation for the owner(s) of an LLC.

Loyalty duty—the duty of members of the board of directors to avoid divided loyalties when they are acting as board members on behalf of the corporation.

M

Market capitalization (often, market cap)—the total dollar value of the corporation's outstanding common stock.

Market research—the process of collecting and analyzing data relating to a business's current and potential marketplace.

Market segmentation—the process of dividing customers into various homogeneous groups based on needs, demographics, consuming habits, or some other common factors.

Market share—the percentage of the total revenue of any given market that a single company generates.

Material error—a deficiency in financial controls that is likely to impact earnings reports and stock price.

Merger—a transaction that combines two or more corporations into a single entity.

Mid-cap corporation—a corporation with a market capitalization between $2 billion and $10 billion.

Multi-business corporation—a corporation made up of multiple business units and a corporate center that governs the units.

Multivariate analysis (MVA)—an approach to statistical analysis that takes into account two or more variables, often used in marketing to understand customers.

N

Net income—a firm's "bottom line" calculated by subtracting expenses from revenues for a specified period of time.

Net present value (NPV)—the value of future cash flow stated in current dollars.

Non-executive director—a member of the board who is not currently an executive of the company; may not be classified as independent due to recent connections to the corporation.

O

Officer—a high-level corporate executive empowered by the board to act on behalf of the corporation.

Offshoring—the transfer of some activities in a firm's business model to a subsidiary in another country.

Opportunity cost—the difference between the expected returns from any decision and the expected returns from the next-best alternative decision.

Organic growth—an increase in revenue due to new products developed from within the company in contrast to growth from acquisition.

Outsourcing—the transfer of some activities in a firm's business model to another company.

P

Patent—a form of intellectual property that protects new, useful, and non-obvious inventions.

Patent fence—a strategy in which a company protects a new product by patenting related technologies to prevent a competitor from entering the same market space.

Patent troll—a company that buys up patents for the purpose of threatening lawsuits against alleged infringers.

Performance appraisal—a regularly scheduled, formal assessment of an employee's performance during a specified time period, typically accompanied by direct feedback in the form of an interview conducted by the supervisor.

Person-organization fit—an approach to employee selection that focuses on the individual values and attitudes of applicants.

Person-task fit—an approach to employee selection that focuses on the particular skills of applicants.

Piercing the corporate veil—an attempt to hold the corporate owner of a subsidiary liable for the actions of that subsidiary.

Place (one of the 4 P's)—the process by which the product gets to the customers; also referred to as distribution.

Plant patent—a patent for a new, distinct, asexually reproducing plant.

Poison pill—a defense against hostile takeovers that involves giving current shareholders the right to purchase additional shares at reduced prices; designed to dilute power of a hostile party.

Preferred stock—a class of stock that comes with no voting rights but is considered a more reliable investment than common stock.

Price (one of the 4 P's)—the terms set for the exchange between the buyer and seller.

Price elasticity of demand—a measure of responsiveness of market demand to changes in the price of a product or service.

Price fixing—a collaboration among firms to set prices for a product or service in a way that contravenes market forces.

Private company—a company that does not offer stock through any public exchange or market.

Private equity firm—a business that uses its capital to purchase an equity position in another company, leverage its influence to make improvements in that company's operation, and sell the equity position for a profit.

Pro forma—a financial statement prepared as part of an intended project or plan involving significant capital expenditure showing its financial impact.

Product (one of the 4 P's)—the offer a company makes to the customer.

Product division—a corporate unit divided up according to the products for which it is responsible.

Profit center—a business unit for which profit and loss is calculated.

Promotion (one of the 4 P's)—activities undertaken to increase awareness, acceptance, and purchase of a product or brand.

Public company—a company that offers its stock to the public through an open exchange or market.

Public Company Accounting Oversight Board (PCAOB)—a nonprofit corporation created by Congress to oversee the implementation of SOX.

Public float—the value of stock owned by the public rather than by directors and executives.

Q

q-ratio—a calculation for determining if a firm is undervalued or overvalued.

R

Related diversification—a corporate strategy that involves moving into other businesses in the same industry.

Relationship marketing—placing an emphasis on maintaining a long-term relationship with a customer.

Research and development (R&D)—the function in business responsible for developing new products and services.

Retained earnings—the sum of every dollar a company has earned since its inception minus all payments made to shareholders.

Retention bonus—a contract in which the bidder agrees to pay a bonus to designated employees at the target if they stay with the bidder for a predetermined amount of time.

Revenue—payments received or expected in exchange for goods and services.

Revenue model—the method by which a business converts its product/service offer into revenue.

Revenue recognition—the accounting of revenue during a specific time period.

Risk—the impact of uncertainty on outcomes.

Risk capacity—the level of risk a corporation can absorb based on available capital.

Risk tolerance—the attitude of board members and executives toward how close to risk capacity the corporation can operate.

Road show—the practice of making formal presentations to important potential investors as part of the IPO process.

S

S-1—a required filing with the SEC in which private firms seek approval to make a public stock offering.

Salary—the annual income associated with a job contingent on the fulfillment of the employment contract.

Sales channel—the firms involved in moving a product from the originating company to the end purchaser.

Sarbanes-Oxley Act (SOX)—2002 legislation that combines risk management with governance and regulatory compliance.

Say on pay—a requirement that corporations allow shareholders to take non-binding votes on board-approved executive compensation plans.

Scenario planning—the process of applying computerized models based on past events in order to understand what impact those events would have on the current organization.

S-Corporation (often, S-Corp)—a corporate form with a tax structure that allows profits and losses to be passed on to shareholders, the issuance of only one class of stock, and with no more than 100 shareholders.

Screen (also, ethical screen)—an information barrier designed to protect against information leakage between competitiors who are also engaged in collaborative action.

Security—a financial instrument (stock, bond, bank note, or other investment contract) that a corporation uses to gain access to capital.

Securities and Exchange Commission (SEC)—the federal agency responsible for protecting investors, maintaining capital markets, and overseeing the sale of securities by public companies.

Segmental financing—the practice of a subsidiary seeking its own financing independent of the corporate parent.

Shared service—a function common to multiple divisions within the corporation that can be centralized to take advantage of the economies of scale.

Shareholders (also, stockholders)—individuals and institutions that share ownership of a corporation by virtue of owning stock.

Shareholders' equity—the value of the firm once all obligations have been met.

Shark repellent—a defense against hostile takeovers that involves bylaws that make it difficult for a hostile party to gain control of a board.

Sherman Antitrust Act (1890)—prohibits anti-competitive agreements and actions.

Silent period—a legally enforceable ban on advocacy by the company or its representatives that occurs during the IPO process.

Small-cap corporation—a corporation with a market capitalization under $2 billion.

Solid-line relationship—a direct reporting relationship between two individuals.

Statement of shareholders' equity—a required financial statement that details all changes in equity.

Stock—a form of ownership or equity in a corporation.

Stock options—a form of reward in which the corporation gives employees the right to purchase stock under specified conditions.

Stock repurchase (also, share buyback)—a purchase by the corporation of its own stock from current shareholders.

Strategic innovation—significant changes in a business's who/what/how strategy.

Strategy—an overview of how a business will compete, grow, and make a profit.

Subsidiary—a business whose stock is owned either completely or mainly by a multi-business corporation and retains a distinct legal structure.

Succession planning—a review of managers, accompanied by developmental plans, to identify individuals who can move into executive positions.

Supervision duty—the duty of members of the board of directors to make sure that corporate executives are complying with relevant laws and regulations when they are acting as board members on behalf of the corporation.

SWOT analysis—a strategic analysis of a business's strengths, weaknesses, opportunities, and threats.

Synergy—the effect that allows two entities to operate more efficiently after they are combined.

T

Tangible product attributes—the physical characteristics of a product that impact its functionality.

Target—the designation for the corporation that is sought by another corporation (bidder) in an M&A.

10-K—a comprehensive annual report submitted by a public corporation to the SEC.

10-Q—a quarterly report submitted by a corporation to the SEC providing a review of the company's operations.

Tender offer—a public offer made by a bidder to the shareholders of the target corporation to accept the bidder's offer.

Threat of substitution—the likelihood that a business from a different industry might attract customers with a substitute product.

Time value of money—the principle that a dollar received today is more valuable than the same dollar received in the future.

Top line—a reference to the revenue generated by a corporation.

Trade dress—a category of trademarks that protects distinguishable, nonfunctional design.

Trade secret—a form of intellectual property that includes confidential and useful information that has been protected by its owner.

Trademark—a form of intellectual property that protects symbols used to differentiate one product or service from another.

Transaction marketing—an approach to marketing that emphasizes a single sale to a specific customer.

Transfer pricing—the rate of exchange, often stated in nonmonetary terms, attached to the movement of goods across units within the same corporation.

Treasury stock—equity held by the corporation as a result of a stock buyback that can be resold in the future.

Triple bottom line—the concept that businesses can take social, ecological, and economic outcomes into equal account.

U

Underwriter—a bank or consortium of institutions that conducts the financial aspects of an IPO, including setting the initial stock price and arranging for buyers.

Unrelated diversification—a corporate strategy that involves moving into other businesses in a different industry.

Upside risk—the potential positive impact of uncertainty on outcomes.

Utility patent—a patent for a new, useful, and non-obvious process.

V

Value pricing—pricing decisions that start with the value attached to the product by customers.

Vertical integration—a corporate strategy to create value by buying or starting up businesses that complement current businesses.

Vertical price fixing—an arrangement between a supplier and a seller to set prices for a product or service in a way that involves coercion and contravenes market forces.

Volcker Rule—a provision of Dodd-Frank intended to curtail risky investments by financial institutions.

W

Weighted average cost of capital—a calculation that considers how much a corporation pays for access to various sources of capital and the proportion of the firm's total capital coming from those different sources.

White knight—a bidder invited by the target's board to prevent a hostile takeover.

Write-down—a reduction in the value of a corporation's assets due to a loss in their market value.

INDEX

D

Discounted cash flow, 15

Discrimination, 53

Disney Company, 31, 32, 33, 34, 49, 70

Distribution. *See* Place

Diversification strategy, 33–35, 45

Dividends, 2, 3, 14

Division, 39

Divisional structure, 38–40

Doctrine of at-will employment, 53

Dodd-Frank Wall Street Reform and Consumer Protection Act, 84, 95, 96–97, 99

Domestic markets, 36

Dotted-line relationship, 41, 45

Double-entry bookkeeping, 10

Dow Jones Sustainability Index, 44

Dry Max technology, 72

Dual-class shares, 81

Due diligence, 124, 133

Duke Energy Corporation, 127

Dunkin' Donuts, 107

DuPont. *See* E. I. du Pont de Nemours and Company

E

E. I. du Pont de Nemours and Company, 56

Earnings before interest, taxes, depreciation, and amortization (EBITDA), 13

Earnings per share (EPS), 12, 13

EBITDA. *See* Earnings before interest, taxes, depreciation, and amortization

Economic risks, 93

Economies of scale, 123

EDS. *See* Electronic Data Systems

Electronic Data Systems (EDS), 10

Eli Lilly and Company, 115

Embraer S.A., 36

Emergency Economic Stabilization Act, 96, 99

Employee flow
  defined, 56
  examples of personal work-related values, 49
  moving right people into business, 48–51
  moving right people through business, 51–53
  moving wrong people out of business, 53

Employee Retirement Income Security Act (1974), 56

Enron Corporation, 9, 95

Enterprise Rent-A-Car, 128

Enterprise risk, 91

Environmental risks, 93

EPS. *See* Earnings per share

Equal Pay Act (1963), 56

Equity position, 38

Ericsson. *See* Telefonaktiebolaget LM Ericsson Company

Ethical screen, 112

Exchange rate fluctuation, 90

Exclusive dealings, 70

Executive committee, 82, 86

Executive compensation, 84–85

Executive Compensation Disclosure Exchange Act, 84–85

Exercise price, 55

Export, 38

Express warranty, 18

F

Facebook, Inc., 62, 67, 72, 115, 131
Fair Labor Standards Act
    (FLSA), 55, 57
Fannie Mae, 48
FASB. *See* Financial Accounting
    Standards Board
FDI. *See* Foreign direct
    investment
Federal antimonopoly statutes,
    112
Federal Employees'
    Compensation Act (1993), 56
Federal Trade Commission Act
    (1914), 70
Federal Trade Commission
    (FTC), 62, 71
FedStats.gov, 62
Feedback, 52
Fiduciary duty, 80, 85
Fiduciary responsibility, 79, 80
Finances, managing
    looking forward and time
      value of money, 6–7
    opportunity cost, 5
    sources of capital, 1–4
    spending capital, 4–7
    weighing cost of capital, 6
Financial Accounting Standards
    Board (FASB), 8, 15, 55
Financial committee, 98
Financial controls
    compliance and, 93–96
    deficiencies in, 94–95, 101
Financial statements
    balance sheets, 10–11
    income statements, 8–10
    statement of cash flows, 11–12
Firm commitment agreement, 131
Five Forces model, 22–25
Ford Motor Company, 110, 132

Foreign direct investment
    (FDI), 37
Foreign entry, mode of, 38
Foreign markets, 36–38, 45
Form 10-K
    Apple Inc., 97
    Dell statement of board
      responsibility for risk
      management, 98
    Google Inc., 62, 92
    reporting on deficiencies, 96
    reporting risks, 92
Form 10-Q, 93
Form 8-K, 96
Form S-1, 129–130, 134
Forward integration, 33, 45
4 P's of marketing, 73
    overview of, 64–65
    place, 69–70
    price, 67–69
    product, 65–67
    promotion, 70–72
Franchising, 37, 38
FTC. *See* Federal Trade
    Commission
FTSE4Good Index, 44
Fuji Xerox Co., Ltd., 37
Future cash flow, 15

G

GAAP. *See* Generally accepted
    accounting principles
Gap Inc., 31, 34, 66, 122
GC. *See* General counsel
GE Appliances, 60
GE Aviation, 60
General counsel (GC), 40, 82
General Electric Company, 31,
    35, 60, 70, 132
General Motors Company,
    30, 35

Intellectual property (*continued*)
  obtaining, 110–113, 116
  overview of, 103
  patent trolls, 109
  patents, 104–105
  protections, 108
  purchasing, 112
  role of, 116
  selling, 114–115
  sharing, 117
  strategic options for,
    110–113, 117
  trade secrets, 107–108
  trade secrets vs.
    patents, 108
  trademarks/trade dress,
    106–107
  types of, 104, 116
  use of, 113–116
  value of, 109–110, 116
Interests dimension, 61
Interface Global Inc., 25, 41,
    42, 43
International Financial
    Reporting Standards
    (IFRS), 8
Internet, 62
Investment contracts, 4
Investors, 4, 5, 33
Investors, thinking like, 14
IP. *See* Intellectual property
iPhone, 33
(IPOs). *See* Initial public
    offerings
Izod, 70

J

Joint development agreements,
    111
Joint ventures, 37, 38
Junk bonds, 4

K

Keebler Company, 121, 122
Kellogg Company, 121, 122
Key words, 135–149
Kmart, 25

L

Lacoste, 70
Large market capitalization
    (large-cap), 32
Layoffs, 53
LBO. *See* Leveraged buyout
Lead director, 83
Legal counsel, 73
Legal process outsourcing
    (LPO), 20
Leveraged buyout (LBO), 128
Liabilities, 10
Licensing
  intellectual property,
    113, 116
  strategy, 37, 38
Limited Liability Companies
    (LLCs), 32
Liquidity, 11
Liquidity ratio, 13
Litigation, 80
LLCs. *See* Limited Liability
    Companies
Low-cost strategy, 25, 27
Low initial pricing, 68
Loyalty duty, 80, 85
Loyalty programs, 64
LPO. *See* Legal process
    outsourcing

M

M-form corporations, 31
Making, intellectual property,
    111, 116

Succession planning, 53
Sunk costs, 6
Supervision duty, 80, 85
Suppliers, 18, 23
Sustainability
    business case for, 42–43
    corporate strategies, 41–44
    measuring green performance,
        43–44
SWOT Analysis. *See* Strengths,
    Weaknesses, Opportunities,
    and Threats Analysis
Synergy, 34

T

Tangible product attributes,
    66, 74
Target, 120
Target markets
    identifying, 18–19, 29, 61–63,
        72, 73
    reaching with 4 P's of
        marketing, 64–72
TARP. *See* Troubled Asset Relief
    Program
Technical skills, 51, 57
Telefonaktiebolaget LM Ericsson
    Company, 36
Threats, 24, 27
Time value of money, 6–7, 15
T.J. Maxx, 39, 40, 123
TJX Companies, Inc., 31, 33, 34,
    39, 40, 123
Top line, 42
Toyota Motors, 111
Trade secrets, 107–108
Trademarks/trade dress,
    106–107, 116
Transfer pricing, 35
Treasury stock, 12

Triple bottom line, 43
Troubled Asset Relief Program
    (TARP), 83
Tudor, Frederick, 21
Twitter Inc., 62

U

Underwriter, 130–131
Uniform Commercial Code, 19
Uniform job classification
    system, 55
Uniform Trade Secrets Act, 107
Uniformed Services Employment
    and Reemployment Rights
    Act (1994), 50
Union Carbide Corporation, 42
United Services Automobile
    Association, 63
Unrelated diversification, 35, 45
U.S. Census Bureau, 62
U.S. Consumer Product Safety
    Commission (CPSC), 72
U.S. Copyright Office, 105
U.S. Department of the
    Treasury, 48
U.S. Food and Drug
    Administration (FDA), 71
U.S. Patent and Trademark
    Office (USPTO), 105, 114
U.S. Securities and Exchange
    Commission (SEC)
    accounting standards and, 8
    compliance requirements, 7
    definition of merger, 120
    on executive compensation, 84
    Form 10-K, 62, 92, 93
    Form 10-Q, 93
    Form 8-K, 96
    Form S-1, 129–130, 134
    on initial public offerings, 128

ABOUT THE AUTHOR

Bert Spector is a Professor of Strategy at Northeastern University and an award-winning author and internationally recognized expert in organizational change and leadership. He has authored and co-authored numerous books, including *Managing Human Assets, Human Resource Management: A General Manager's Perspective, The Critical Path to Corporate Renewal,* and *Taking Charge and Letting Go.* His articles have appeared in the *Harvard Business Review* and the *Sloan Management Review.* His best-selling change management textbook, *Implementing Organizational Change: Theory into Practice,* is currently in its third edition. Spector has been a visiting professor at INSEAD and the MIT Sloan School of Management. His extensive executive training and development activities have included engagements with law firms and corporations on both sides of the Atlantic. For four years, he was the faculty coordinator for the FBI's emerging executives program.